FAITH MOVES **MOUNTAINS**

30 Devotional Thoughts to Inspire Your Journey of Faith

by Stephen Cook

Dedicated to:
My most loyal and encouraging fan and the one who gave me the
inspiration for creating this book

"Happy Mother's Day"

Come join me on this journey and discover what it can mean to
walk by faith and not by sight.

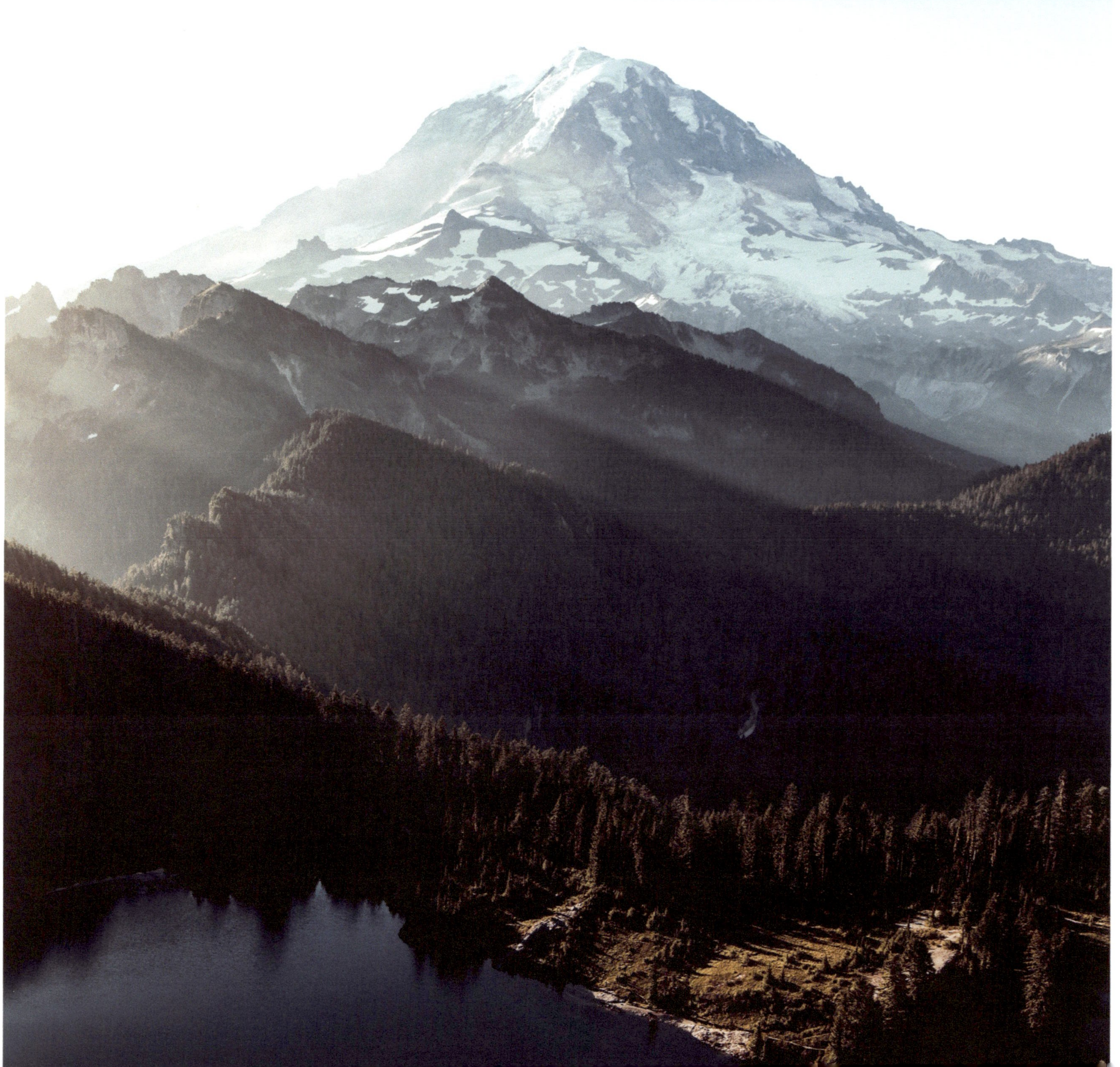

INTRODUCTION

Hebrews 11:1, 3, 6
"Now faith is the substance of things hoped for, the evidence of things not seen.
By faith we understand that the worlds were framed by the word of God, so that the things which are seen were not
made of things which are visible. But without faith it is impossible to please Him, for he who comes to God must believe
that He is, and that He is a rewarder of those who diligently seek Him."

•

The road in front of us can often become foggy and disorienting, causing us to give way to hopelessness and despair. It is
times like these that we are often presented with the choice to either turnaround and go back to comfort and safety,
linger in a state of loss and hesitation, or press on to discover what lies beyond the fog.
One thing I have learned is that new discoveries and new horizons only come by relentless pursuit, a concept that is
both exhilarating and intimidating, as it has no room for laziness and requires constant self-denial.

There will be times when you feel fear. You will have questions. You will have doubts. But life will not hand you a silver
platter with all your answers neatly arranged on it. So likewise, your faith will never grow unless you put your hand to
the plow and put in the effort. God will meet us in our distresses, but we must always do our part to draw near to Him
and He will also draw near to us. He will always guide our paths, but we must learn to take steps.

We are each created with unique talents and abilities with a purpose to glorify Him, and the only way to discover that
purpose is to relentlessly pursue the One who breathed in us the breath of life.

•

This little book is neither groundbreaking insights nor lengthy rambles about the complexities of life. It is intended to be
a simple collection of photographs, scriptures, and inspirational thoughts, and quotes that I feel appropriately
apply to the photos on display.

The making of this book has taken nothing short of literal blood, sweat, and tears and even jail time as I have hiked to
remote and undisclosed locations, wrestled in my faith, and learned difficult life lessons.

My hope is that this will inspire you on your own journey of faith, to not give up when things are down,
and to have the courage to push your limits as you seek to find and tell your own unique story.

34°43'36"N 83°43'30"W

*"But God clearly shows and proves His own love for us, by the fact that
while we were still sinners, Christ died for us."*
– Romans 5:8 AMP

•

It's a familiar verse for some, but, for me, how it is worded casts a new light on the truth it reveals. Specifically, the word prove is what stands out. Often, when I find myself in life's trying times, it is difficult to make sense of all God's promises when measured against what I see in the physical world and real-life circumstances. I often become frustrated and come to God saying, "prove it!"

...to which, I am reminded that He has nothing left to prove to us. He has already clearly PROVEN His love and faithfulness to us on the cross. While I think it is good to ask God questions and to struggle and grow in faith, it is often easy to fall into the mindset of thinking that he owes us something.

He owes us nothing. We owe Him everything.

In truth, we are here for Him, not the other way around. Perhaps, rather than starting each day with a mindset of asking God to help us get through our day, would it not be better to begin each day with a heart that says,

"Lord, how can I serve you today?"

He is near for our good, but we are ultimately here for His glory. We sometimes feel entitled to receive His gifts and we often look for the fulfillment of His promises in our lives but when all other promises tarry and seem distant, there is still one that remains ever near and ever constant.

There is no promise more precious than the gospel itself

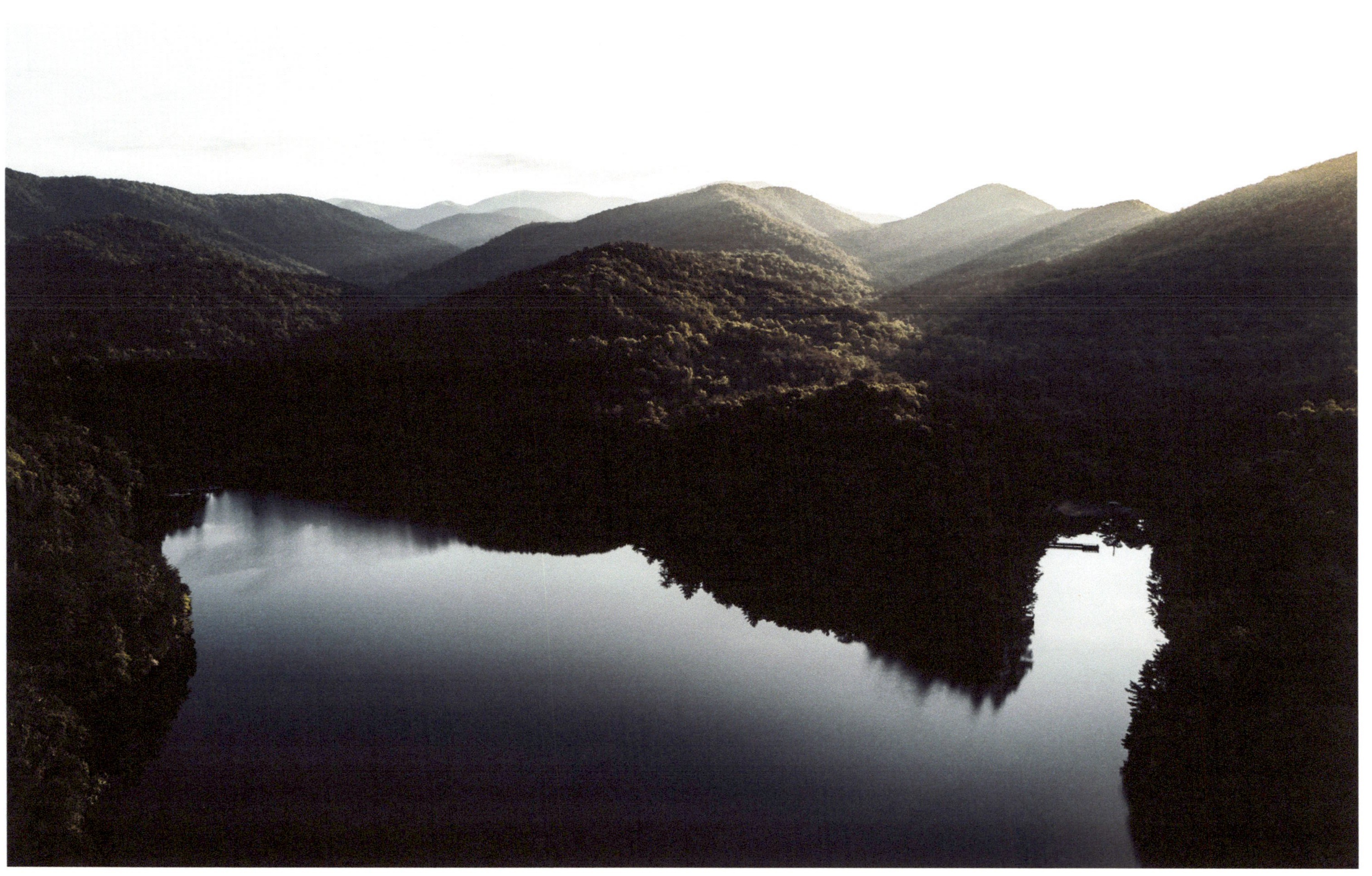

48°03'20"N   123°44'25"W

"Therefore I tell you, do not worry about your life, what you will eat or drink; or about your body,
what you will wear. Is not life more than food, and the body more than clothes? Look at the birds of
the air; they do not sow or reap or store away in barns, and yet your heavenly Father feeds them.
Are you not much more valuable than they?"
– Matthew 6:25-26 NIV

•

He holds everything in His capable hands. He commands the morning and the evening. He lifts all
who are weary and broken and bears the burdens of many. Not a bird falls to the ground without His
knowledge and every nest has His blessing over it.

Will He not also care for you?

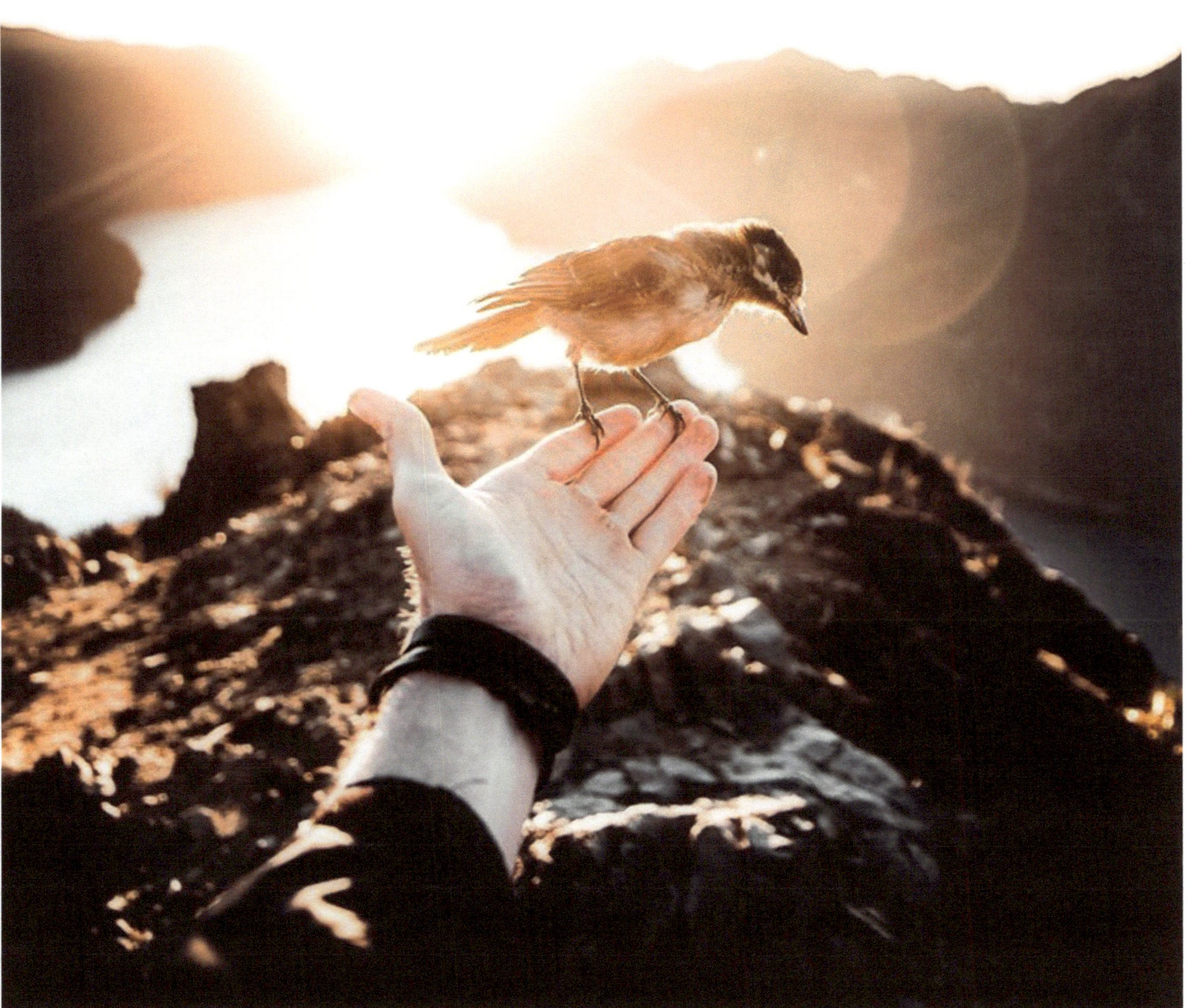

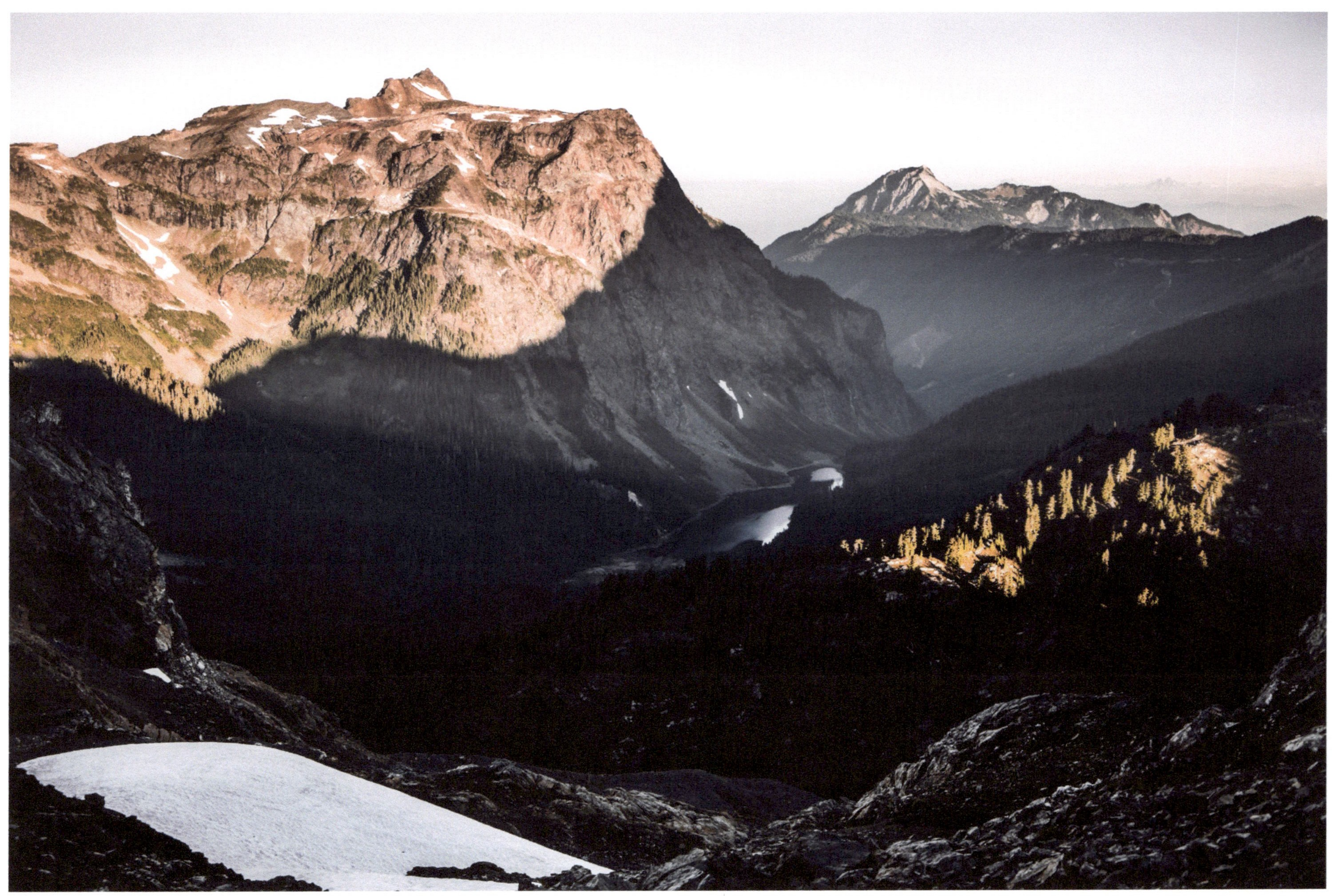

48°57'23"N 121°38'35"W

All things were formed by His hand, and nothing escapes His attention.
The depths of the earth are His, and the mountains. The deepest of valleys
sit quiet and still while the highest of peaks shout His sovereignty.

35°54'49"N   81°53'10"W

"If we imagine we have to put on our Sunday moods before we come near to God,
we will never come near Him. We must come as we are."
— Oswald Chambers

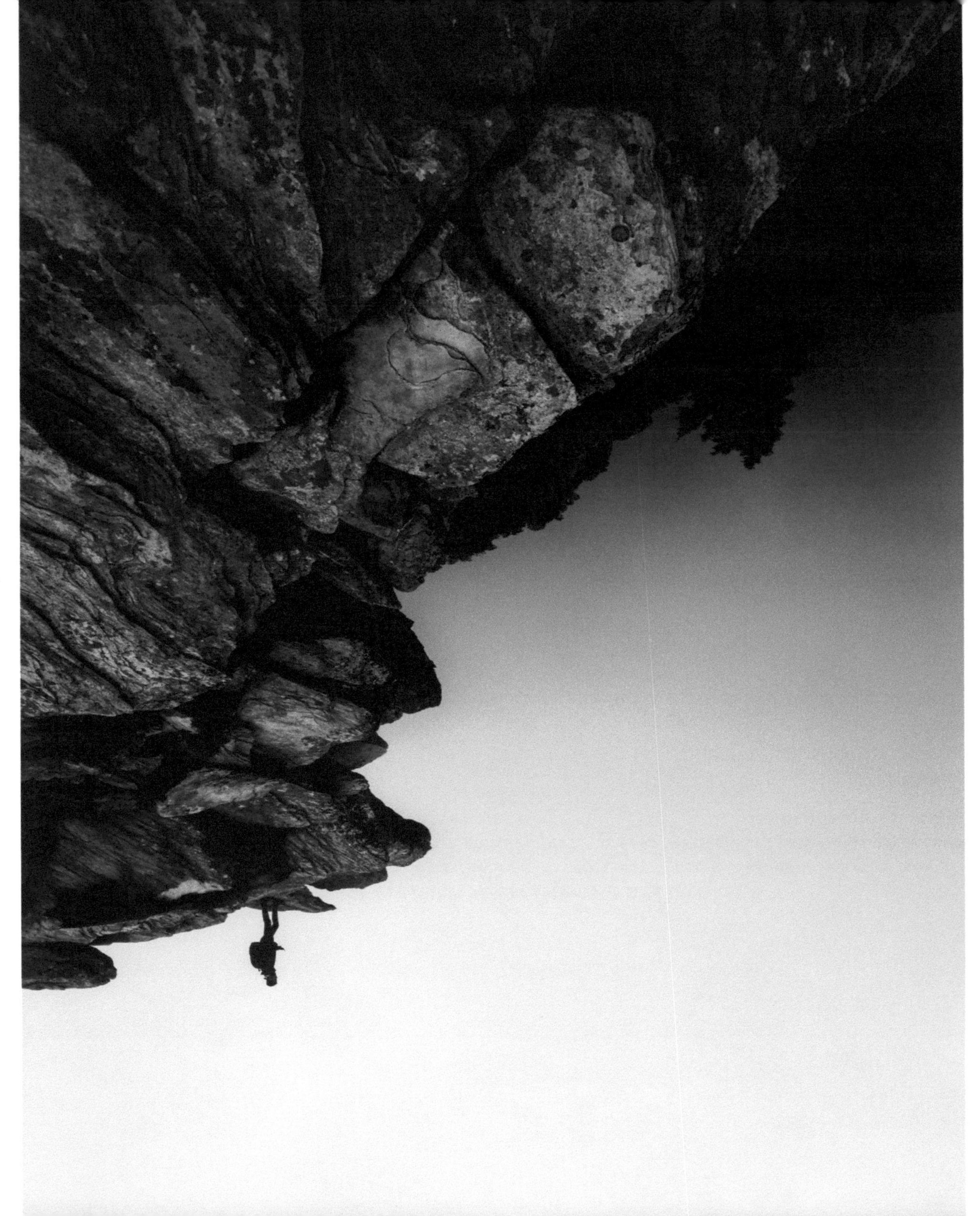

"Love is patient, love is kind. It does not envy, it does not boast,
it is not proud. It does not dishonor others, it is not self-seeking, it is not easily angered, it keeps no record of wrongs.
Love does not delight in evil but rejoices with the truth. It always protects, always trusts, always hopes, always perseveres.
Love never fails..."
— 1 Cor. 13:4-8

•

Have you ever read that through and felt some sense of being overwhelmed by the need to strive to show this love?
I try to live up to this standard and strive to show this love to others but always fall short.

Let me pose to you a simple perspective shift.

In 1 John 4, we're told that God is [agape] love; the same love that is in 1 Cor. 13. We are also taught in scripture that Jesus is the picture and perfection of love.

So, instead of reading 1 Cor. 13 as just another set of things to strive for and fail at, try reading it in this way by replacing the word love with the name of Jesus. Think of it as something that He has already done for you.

"Jesus is patient, Jesus is kind. He does not envy, He does not boast, He is not proud. He does not dishonor others, He is not self-seeking, He is not easily angered, He keeps no record of wrongs. Jesus does not delight in evil but rejoices with the truth. He always protects, always trusts, always hopes, always perseveres.
Jesus never fails."

•

We have only to rest and trust in Him, and He will do the rest through us.

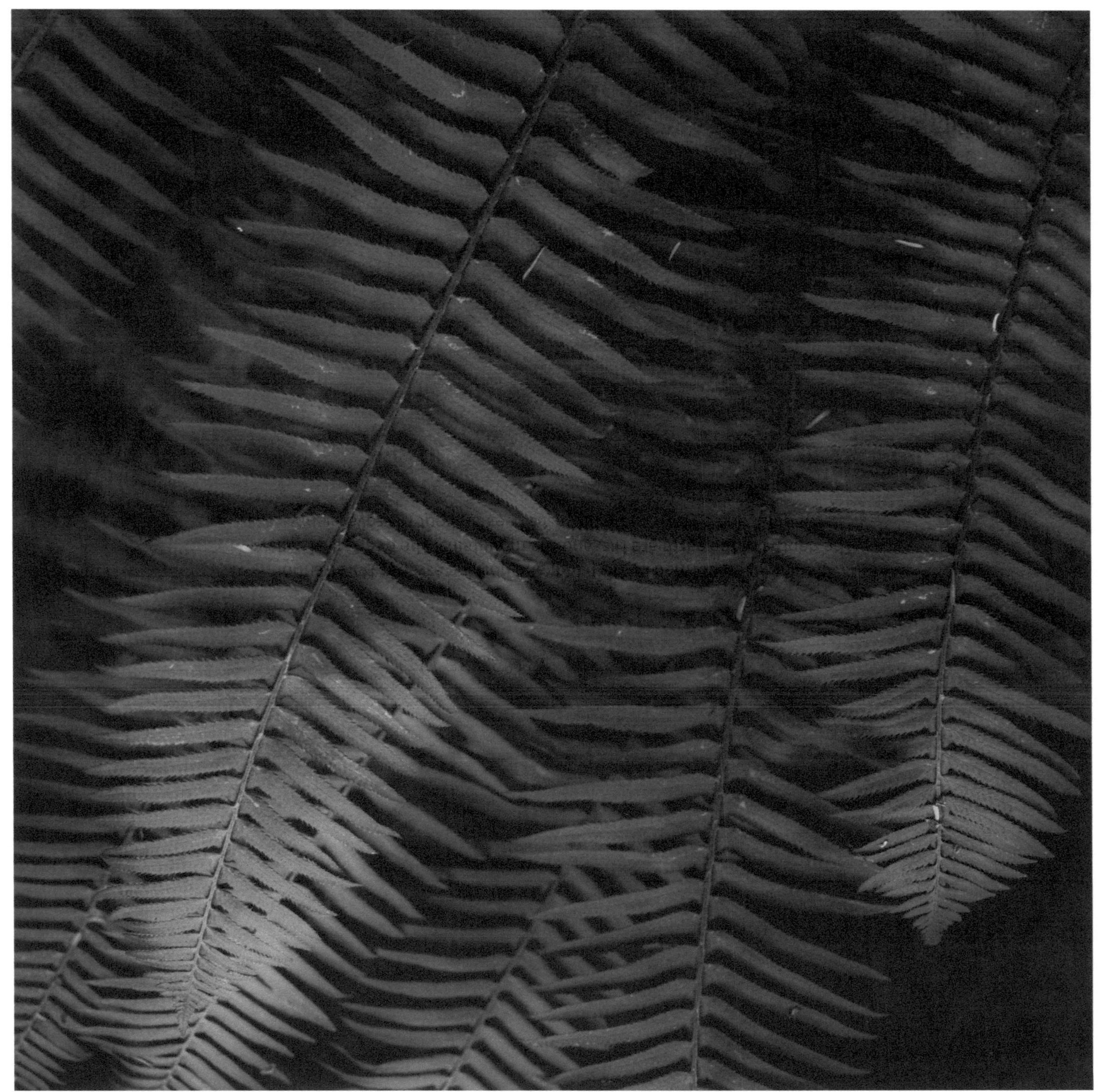

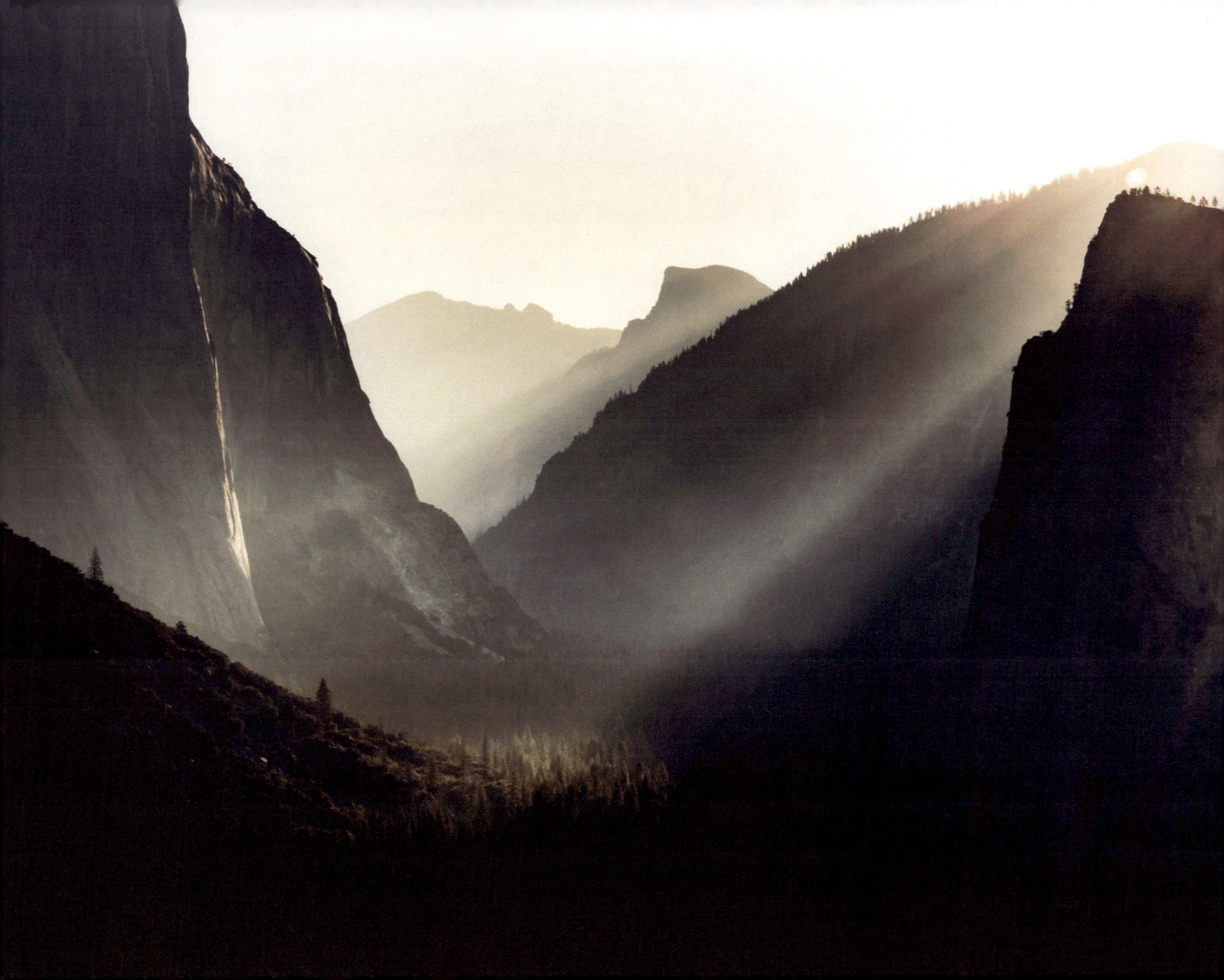

37°42'56"N   119°40'37"W

"In the heartfelt mercy of our God, the dawn from on high will visit us,
to shine on those sitting in darkness, in the shadow of death, to guide
our feet to the way of peace."
– Luke 1:78-79

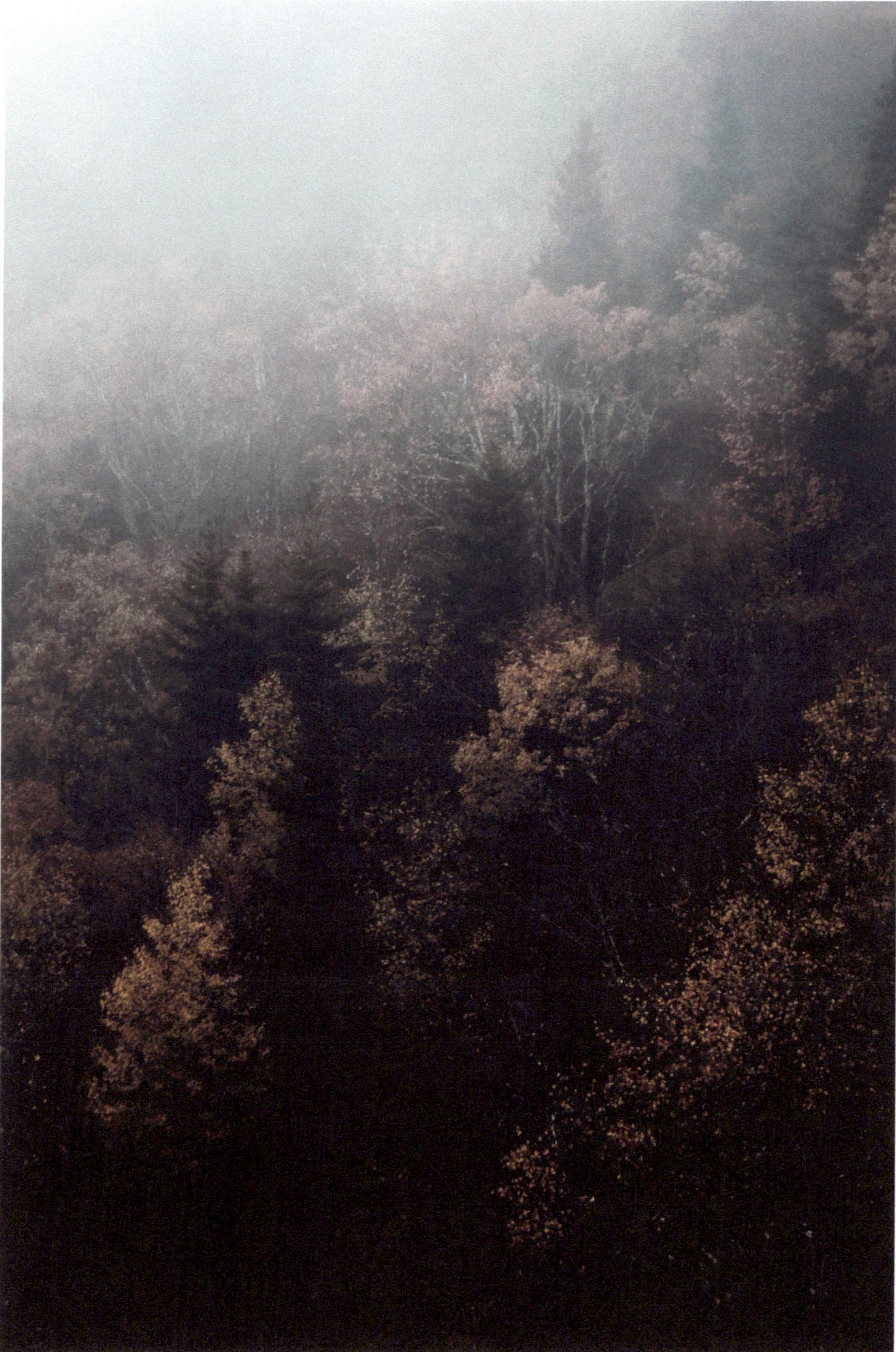

35°21'27"N   82°47'35"W

The In-between

The transition between seasons can often become a
season in and of itself. The old must be shed before the
new can be brought in. Dead things must fall away before
new life can begin.

Yet, we often fail to recognize the beauty in the passing
away because of the pain in the current moment.
The in-between is not a season to dread but a time to embrace and enjoy. There is beauty to be found in
the in-between.

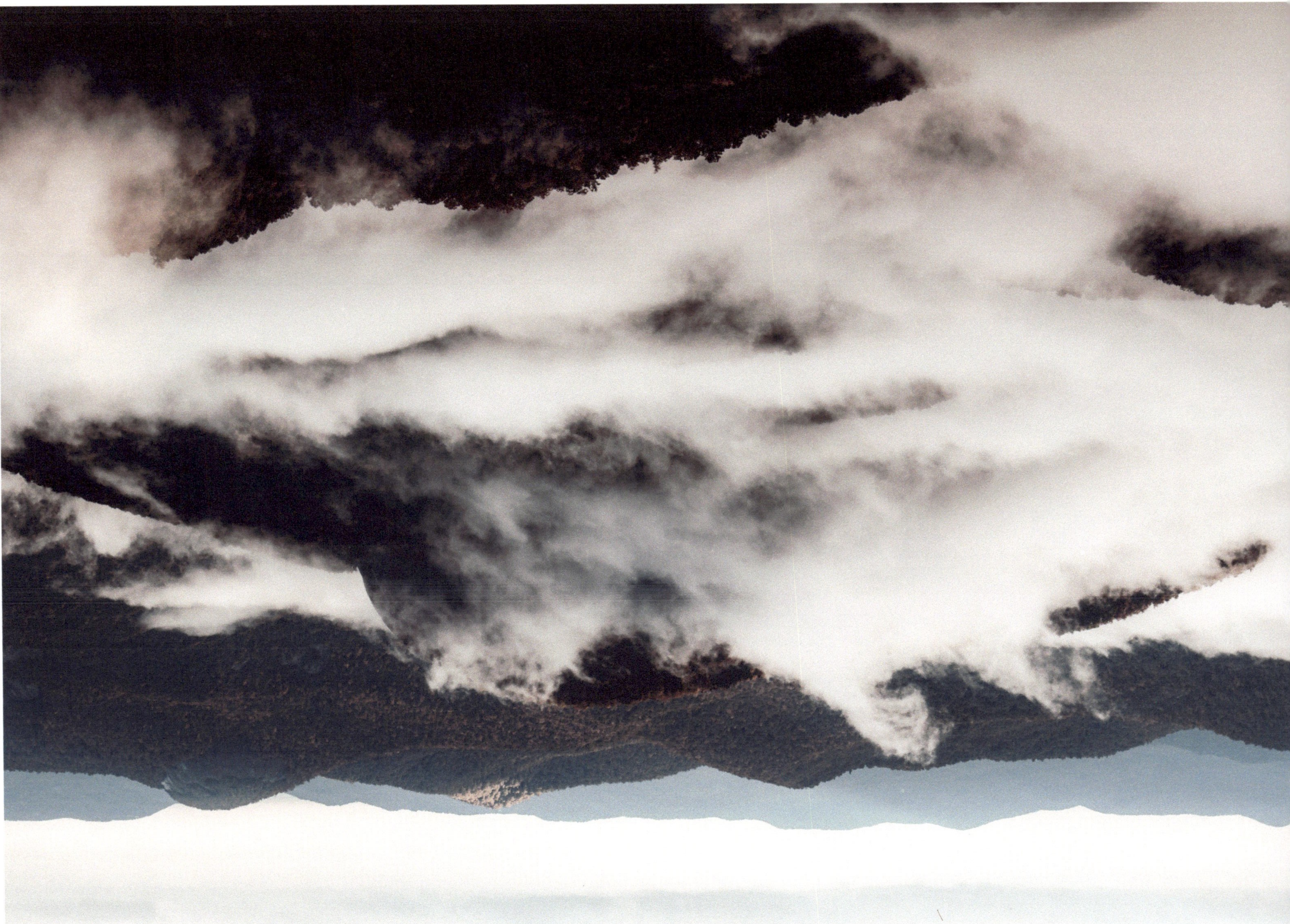

48°03'20"N 123°44'25"W

"The sheep that are My own hear My voice and listen to Me;
I know them, and they follow Me."
— John 10:27 AMP

•

God's voice is tender, still and small, compassionate and forgiving.
It is sometimes easy to miss, but always hard to ignore. When He speaks, He speaks with
compassion and authority, and when He calls you,
He most often calls you by your name.

He is speaking. Are you listening?

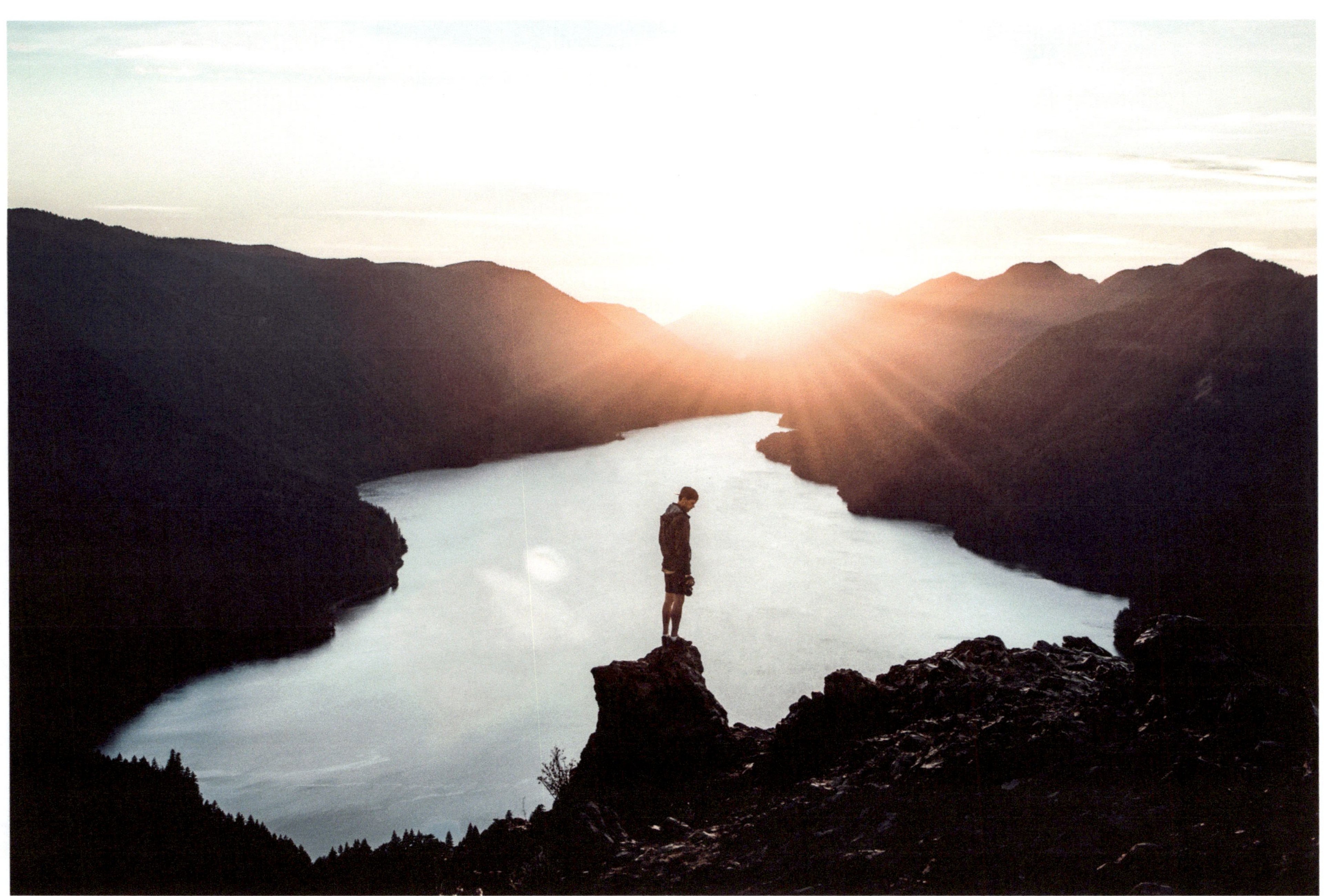

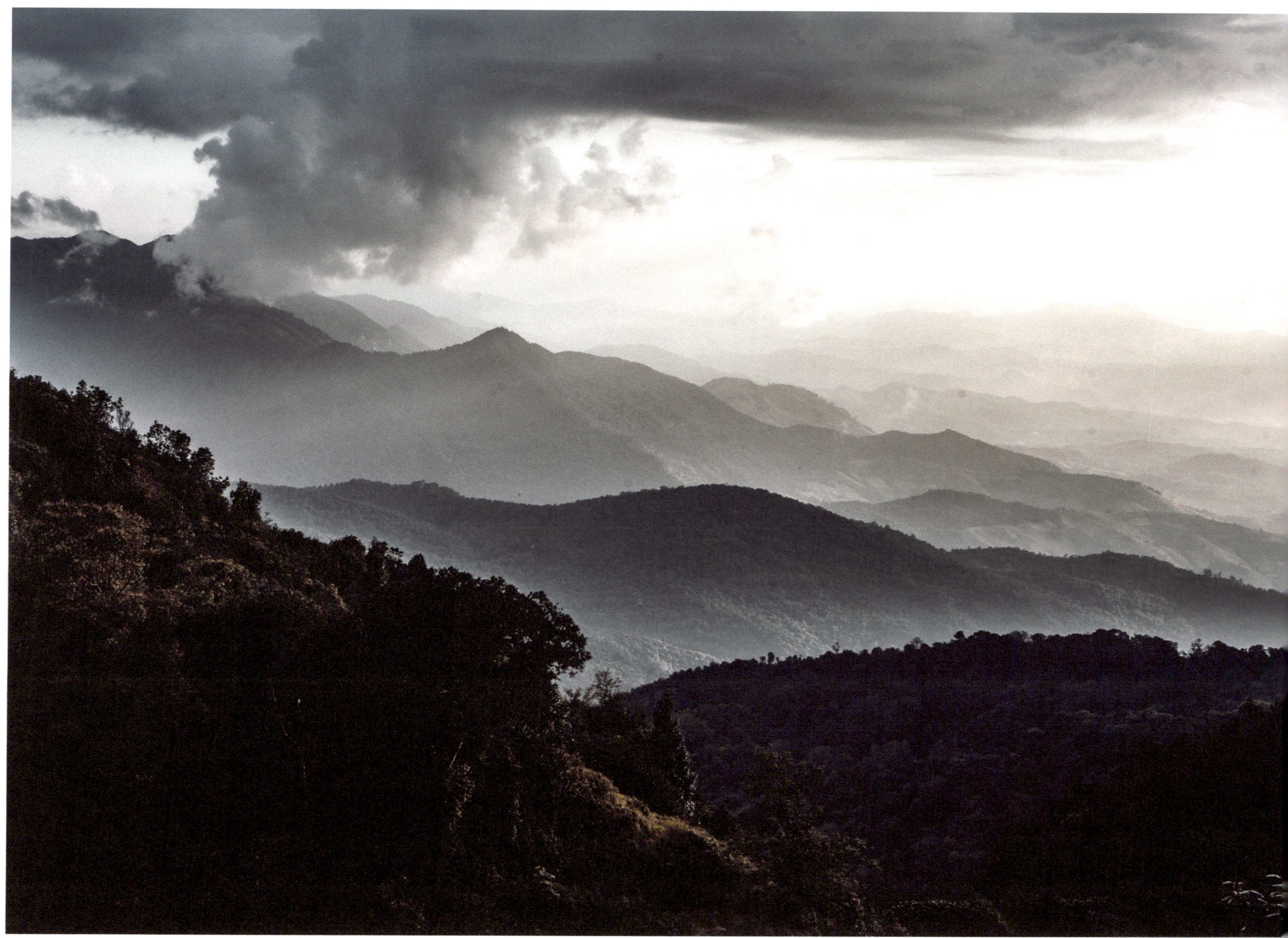

<u>A Prayer for Deliverence</u>

Heavenly Father
Beautiful Savior
I look to You now
My redeemer

Come and save me
From the river
And give me a new hope
That only You can

You're all I have
You're all I need
You came in pow'r
You gave Your all

And now I see
You're everything
Lord Jesus come
Deliver me

And give me grace
To give my all
And all will see
That You are Lord

UNDISCLOSED

"Call to Me, and I will answer you, and show you great and mighty things,
which you do not know."
– Jeremiah 33:3

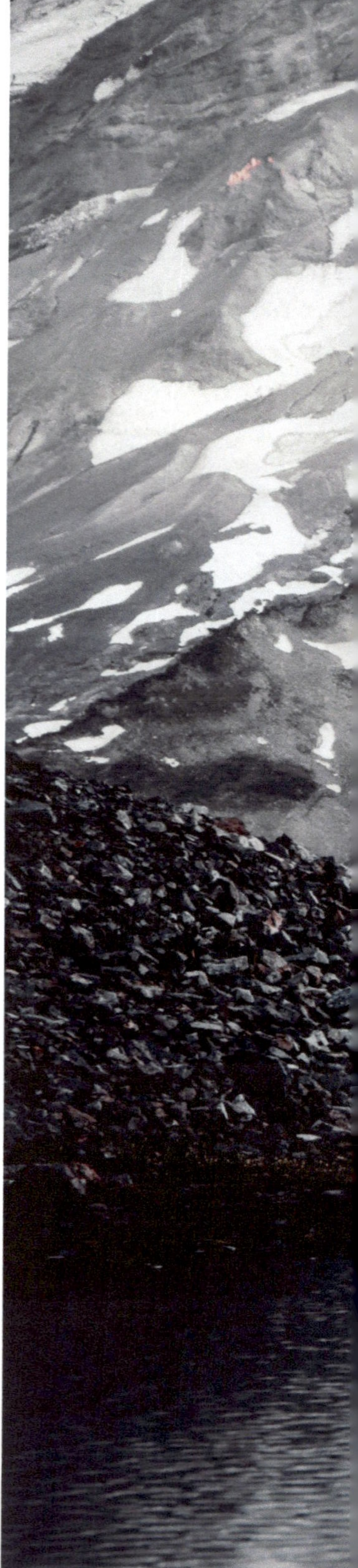

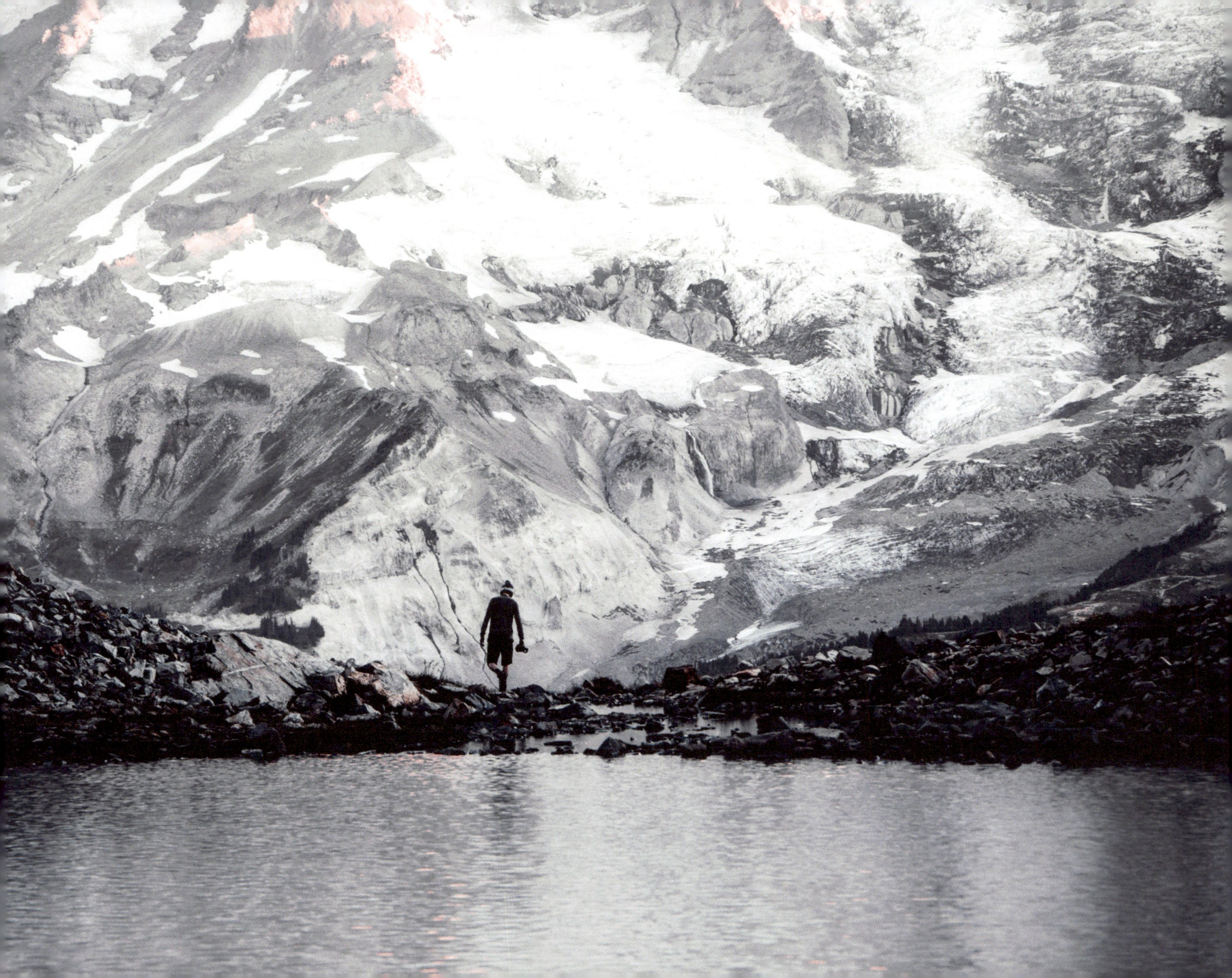

35°39'59"N   85°21'21"W

<u>Courage | Fearlessness</u>

Though they are often seen as synonymous, these words are
NOT interchangeable.

One who is fearless has no need of courage.

Courage always precedes fearlessness. Take heart, keep taking
steps into the unknown, and fearlessness will come.

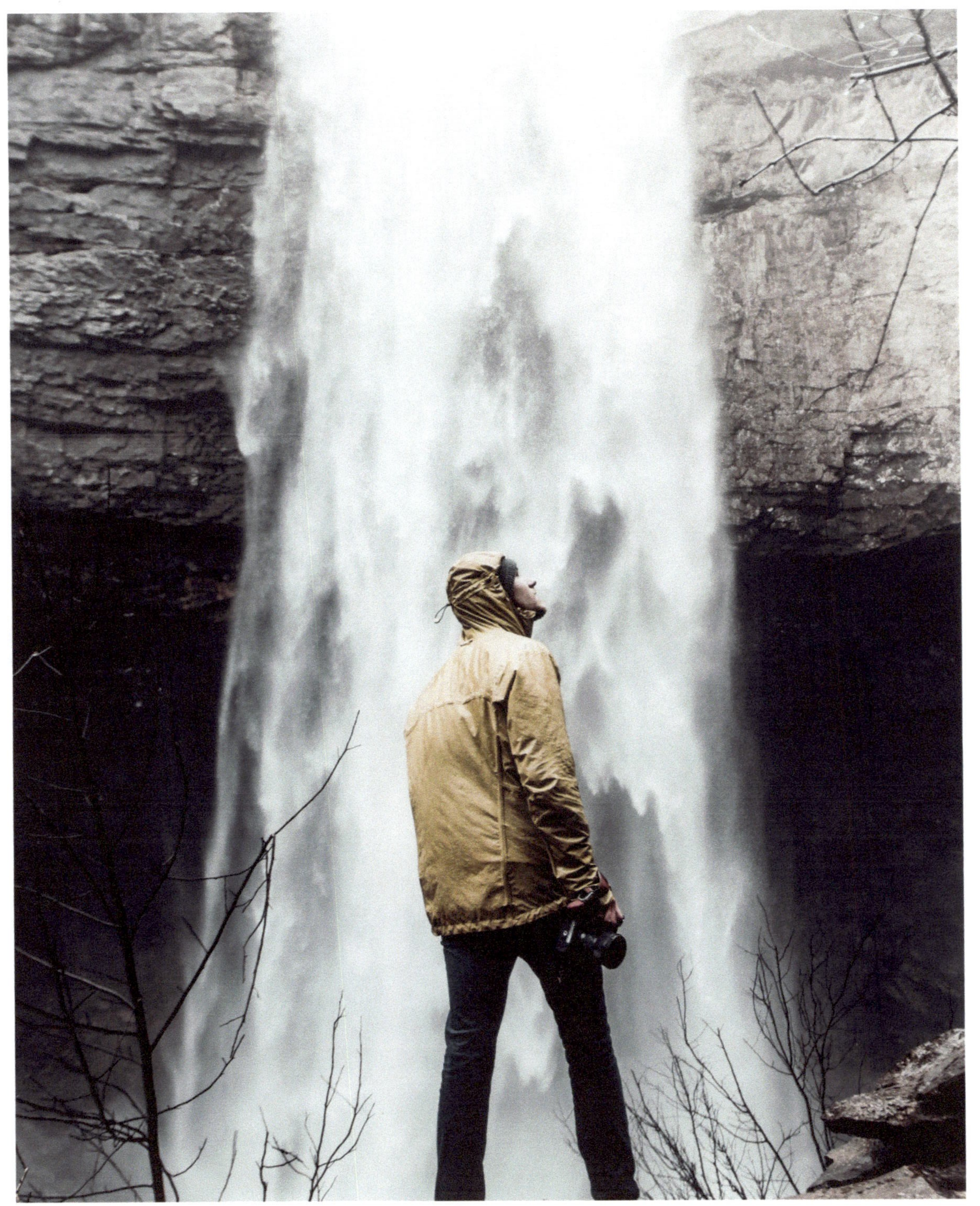

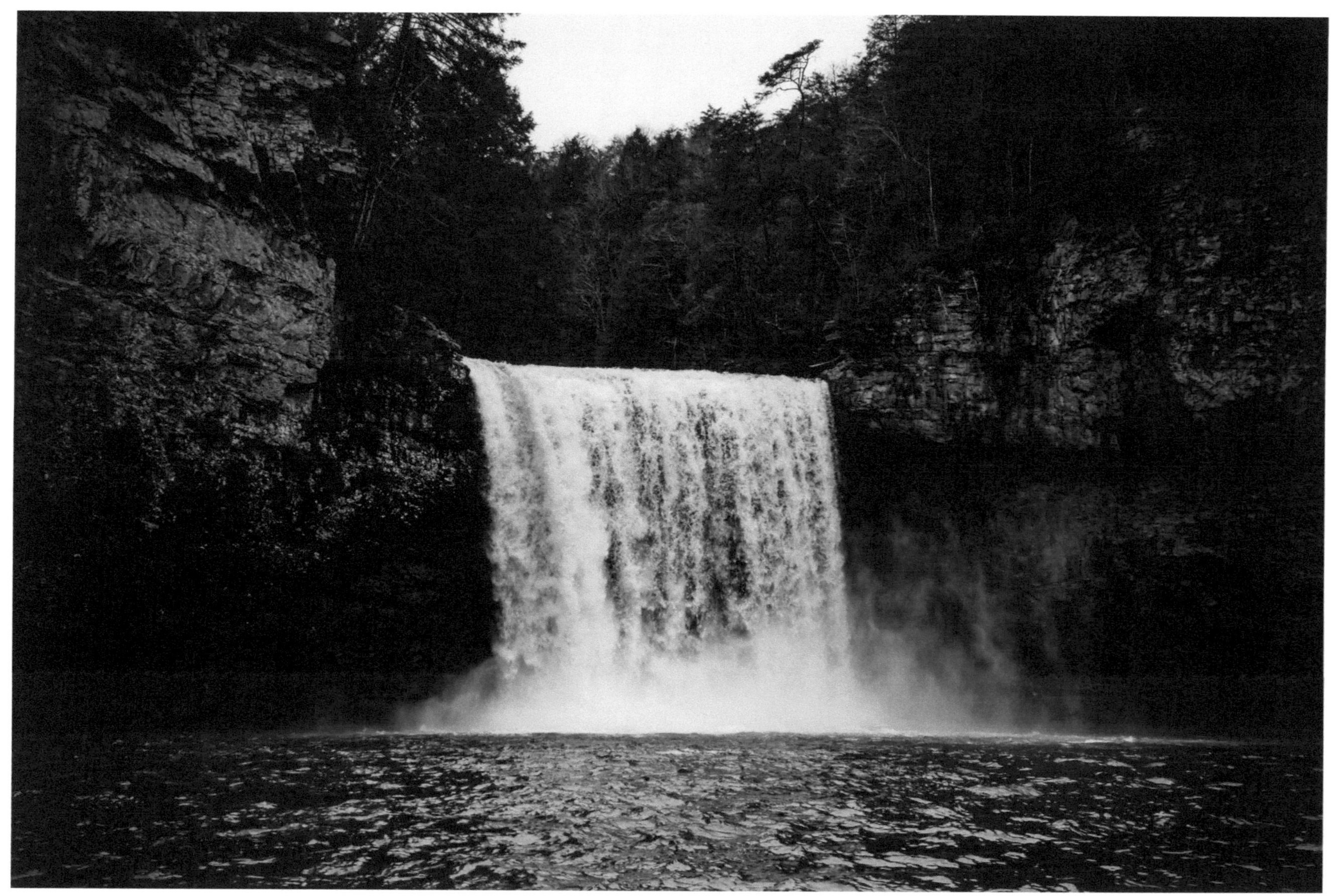

35°39'48"N   85°20'57"W

"Deep calls to deep at the roar of Your waterfalls..."
— Psalm 42:7

•

Typically, when I visit a popular place, I try to find a unique vantage point by looking through branches or by finding an interesting angle with lots of foreground. I try to find the shot that no one else has. However, upon my first time seeing this waterfall I felt that it demanded a kind of "classical" composition with the subject focused in the middle. With its straight lines and even flow, there just didn't seem to be a better way to photograph it.

•

Sometimes, in our search for individuality, we risk skewing the unadulterated truth. It is often best to keep things simple and straightforward by speaking the truth plainly.

Those who seek to save their life will lose it and
those who choose to lose their life for the sake of Christ will find it.
— Matthew 16:25

If you set out to establish your individuality and identity on your own, then you will ultimately lose it.
If you seek to lose yourself in the person of Jesus, then you will ultimately find your identity, and your unique perspective will shine through and thus minister to others.

35°47'47"N   82°57'28"W

"Apart from a personal experience with God and basking in His presence, Christianity does not mean anything. It is just another religion."
– A.W. Tozer

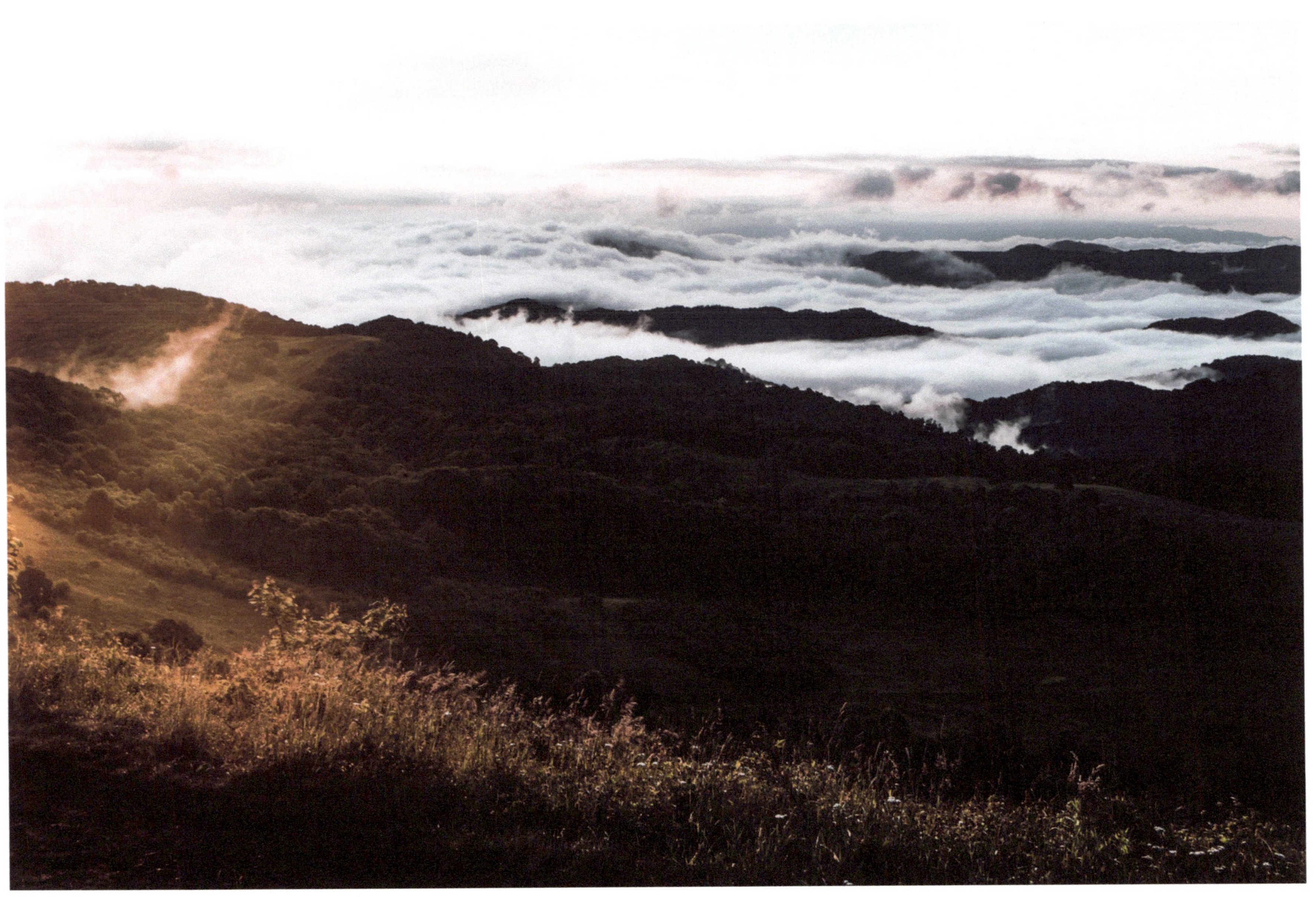

A Hymn of Faith

Though the fig tree bears no fruit and the
grape vines produce no grapes

Though the olive crop fails and the fields
produce no food

Though there are no sheep in the pen and
no cattle in the stalls

Yet I will rejoice in the Lord, I will be joyful in
God my Savior.

Though he slay me, yet will I hope in him

The Sovereign Lord is my strength; he makes
my feet like the feet of a deer, he enables me
to tread on the heights.

Habakkuk 3:17-19 | Job 13:15

•

The true test of faith comes when life
appears fruitless in the areas where we most
want to bear fruit.

It is in this wilderness, of sorts, that we are
tested to see if we are founded
on rock or on sand.

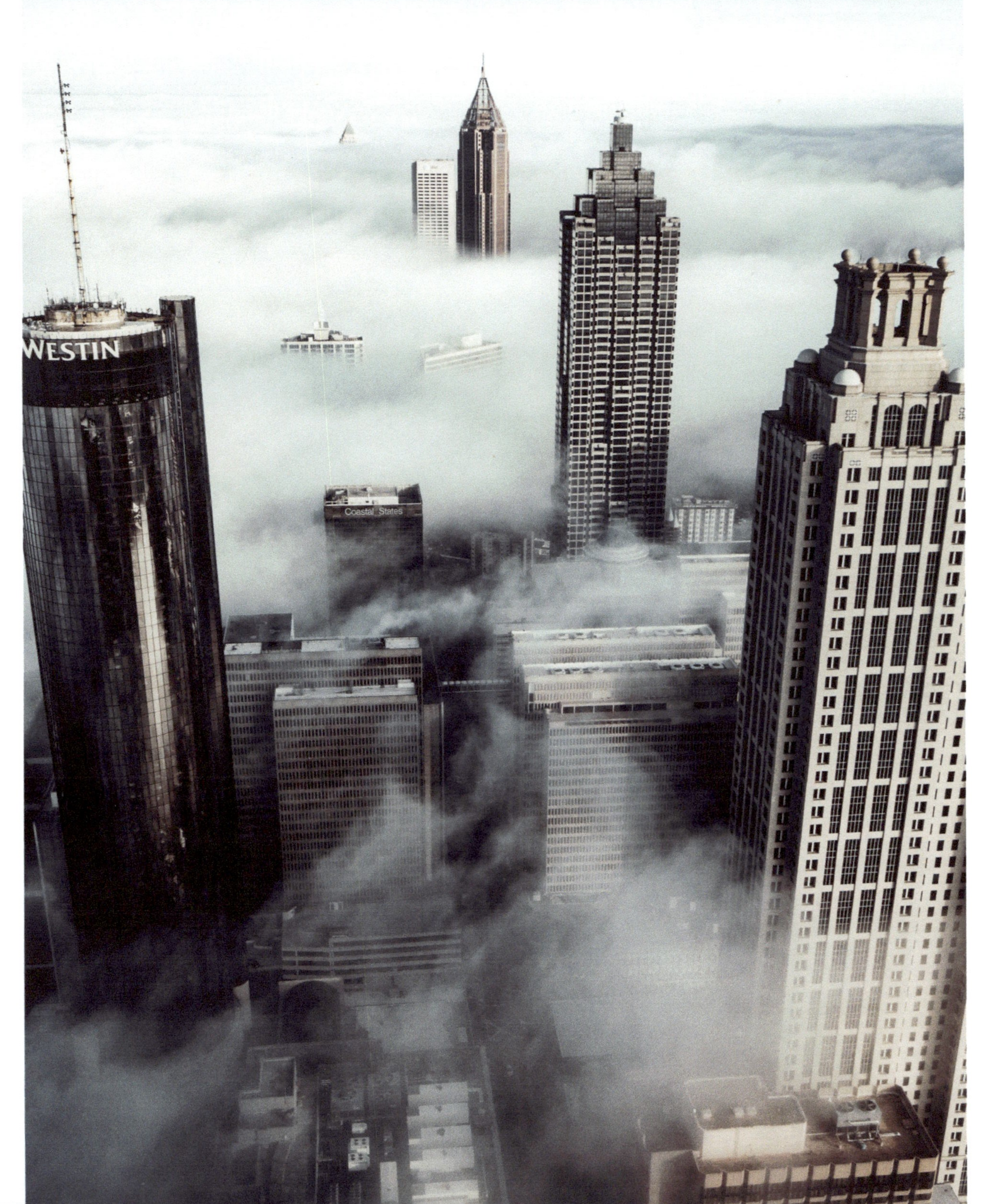

WESTIN
Coastal States

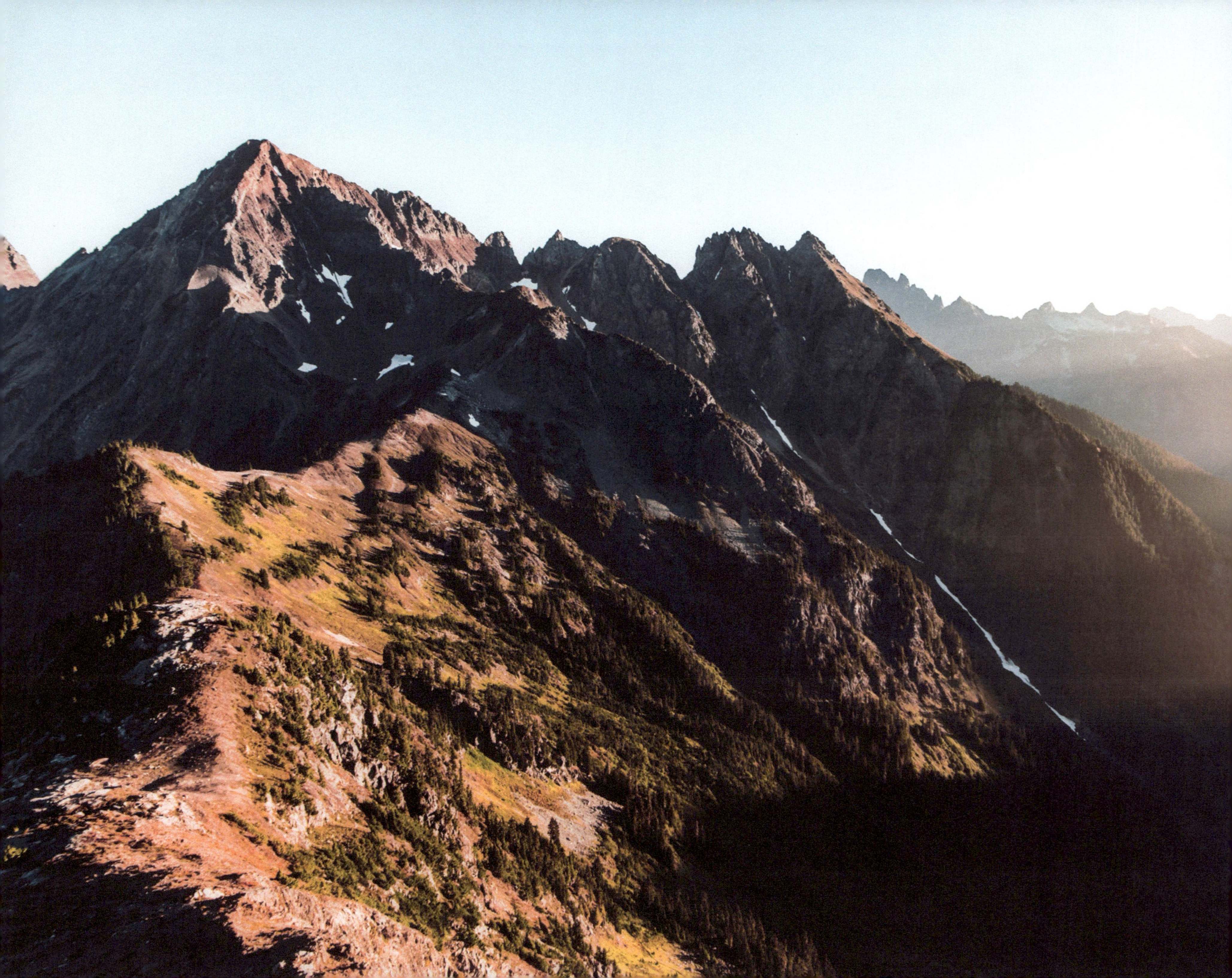

48°57'23"N 121°38'35"W

"Where can I go from your Spirit? Where can I flee from your presence? If I go up to
the heavens, you are there; if I make my bed in the depths, you are there. If I rise on
the wings of the dawn, if I settle on the far side of the sea, even there your hand
will guide me, your right hand will hold me fast."
– Psalms 139:7-10

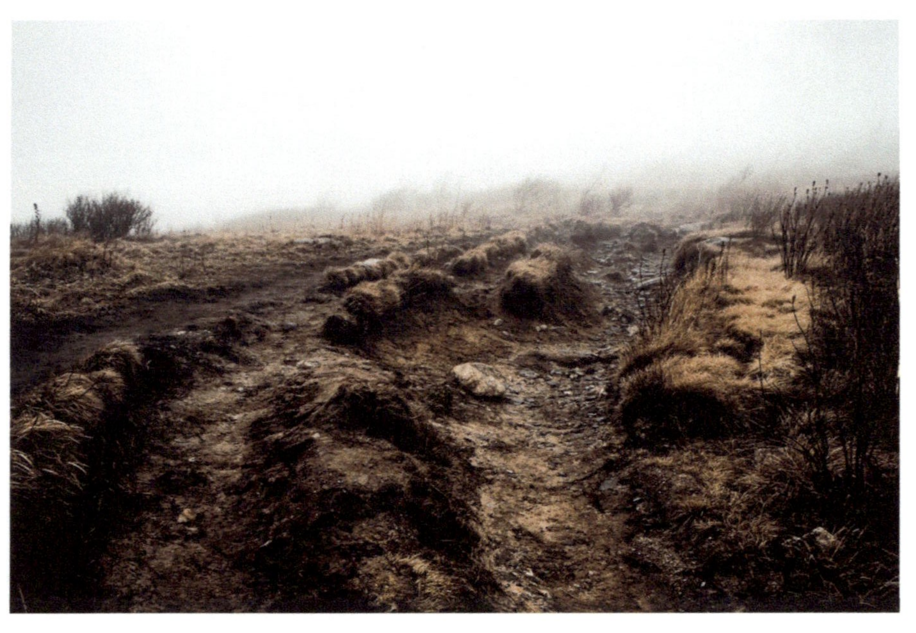 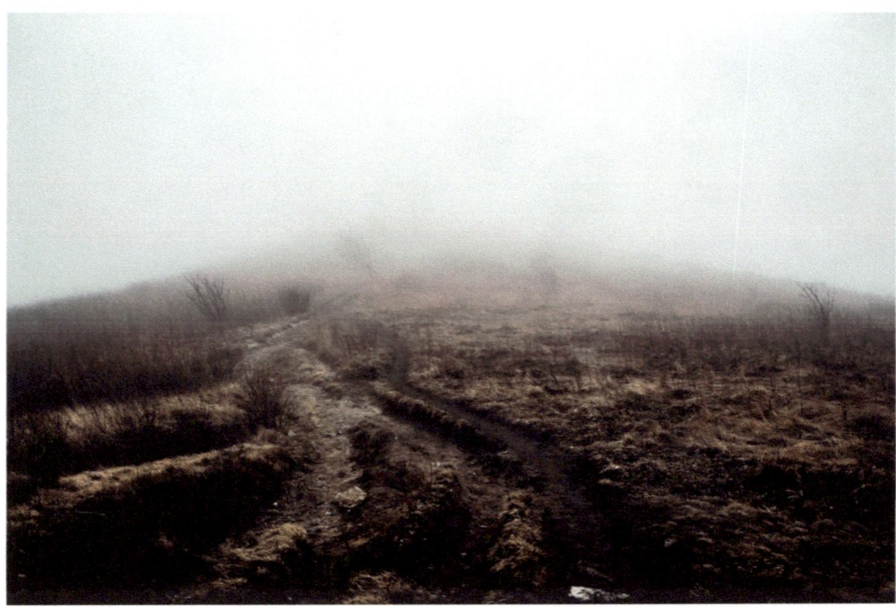

G R I T

When the trail gets rough and clouded,
and we feel lost and confused, there is
only One we can look to for the strength
and courage to press on.

It is during these times of barren land and
uncertainty that we must purpose in our
hearts to continue to just keep taking
the next step.

He does not promise clear and sunny
days, but He does promise to be with us
and give us what we need when we've lost
all desire to keep going.
The clouds will, however, eventually part
and the trail will become smooth again.
Only then will we discover the progress
we've made and the distance
we've traveled.

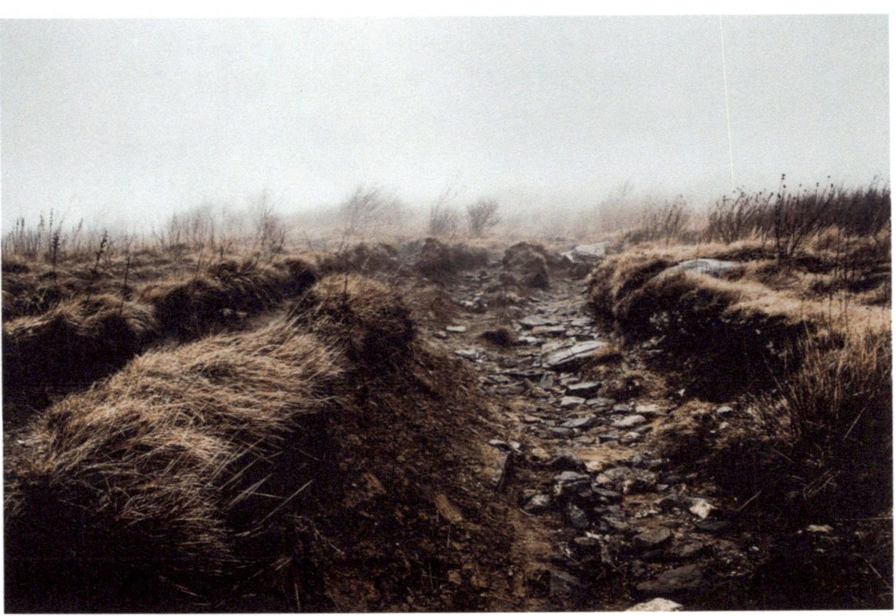

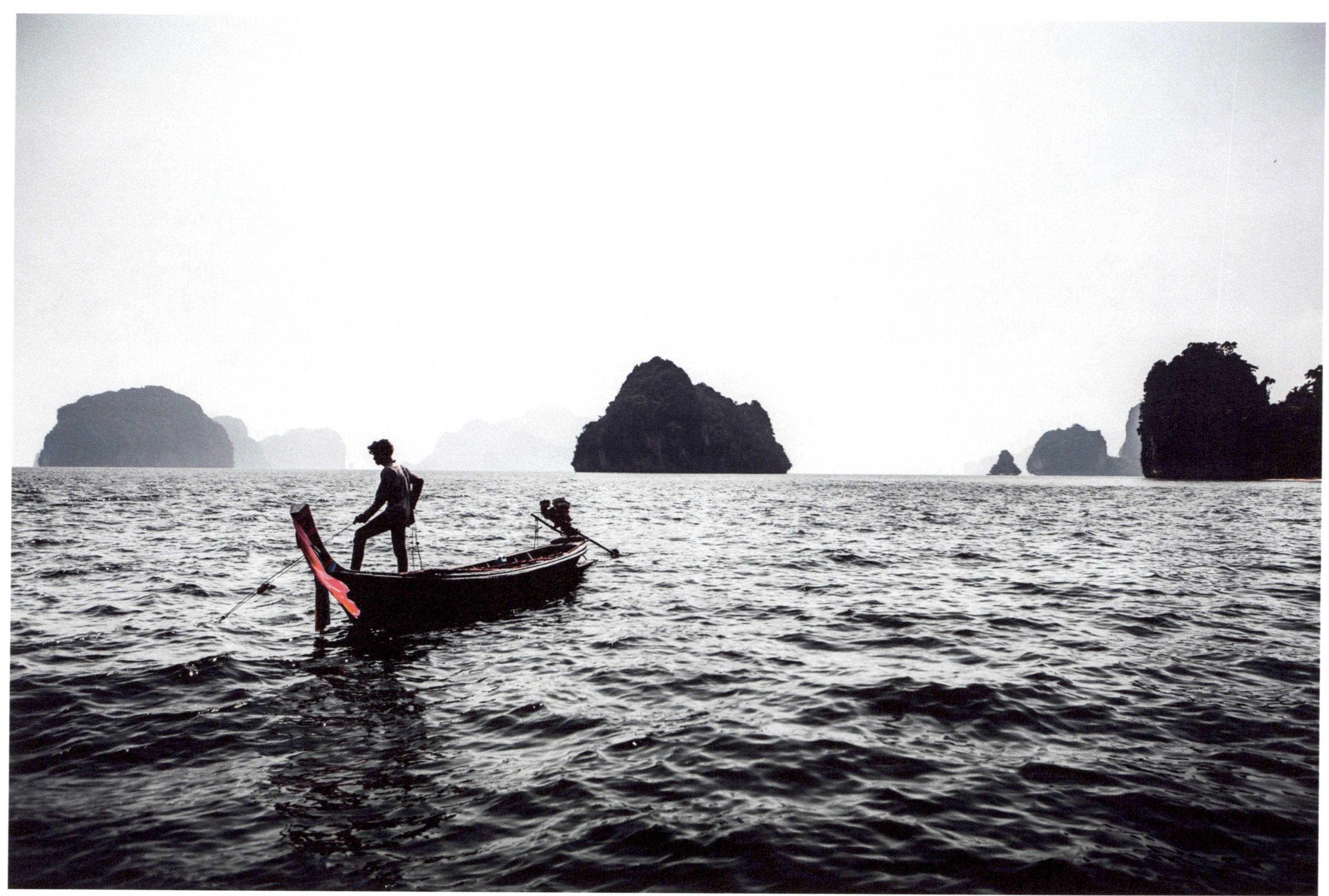

8°15'30"N   98°28'49"E

There is one who gives peace.
There is one who gives rest.

He gives purpose and He gives meaning.

His rivers and His streams speak of His goodness.
His mountains and His valleys declare His praise.

Yet for all the beauty that He's created,
it still falls short of His pride and joy.

His greatest masterpiece happened the
moment you drew your first breath.

37°43'49"N   119°34'25"W

I sought the LORD (Yahweh), and He heard me,
And delivered me from all my fears.

The righteous cry out, and He hears,
And delivers them out of all their troubles.

Many are the afflictions of the righteous,
But the LORD delivers him out of them all.
– Psalm 34:4, 17, 19

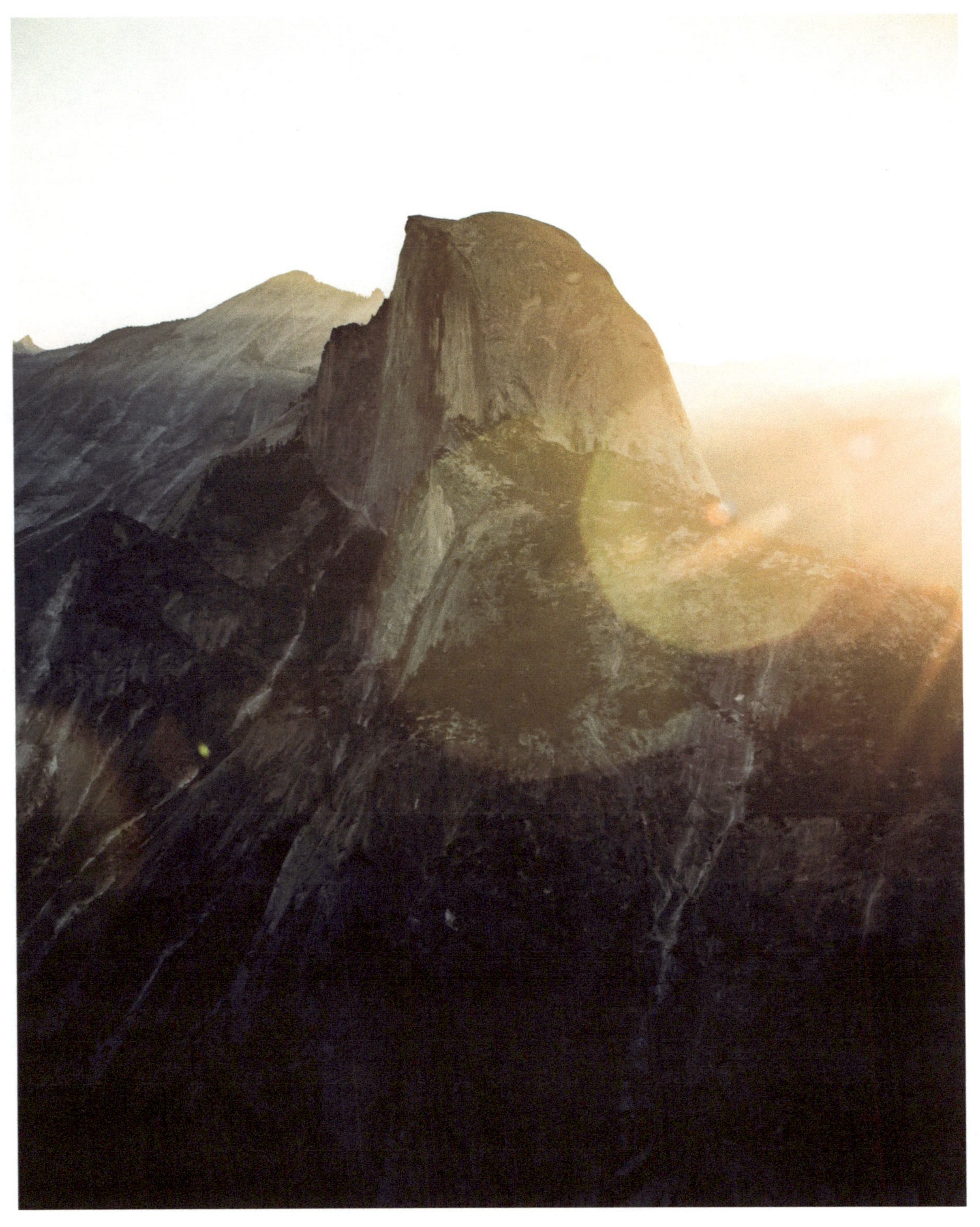

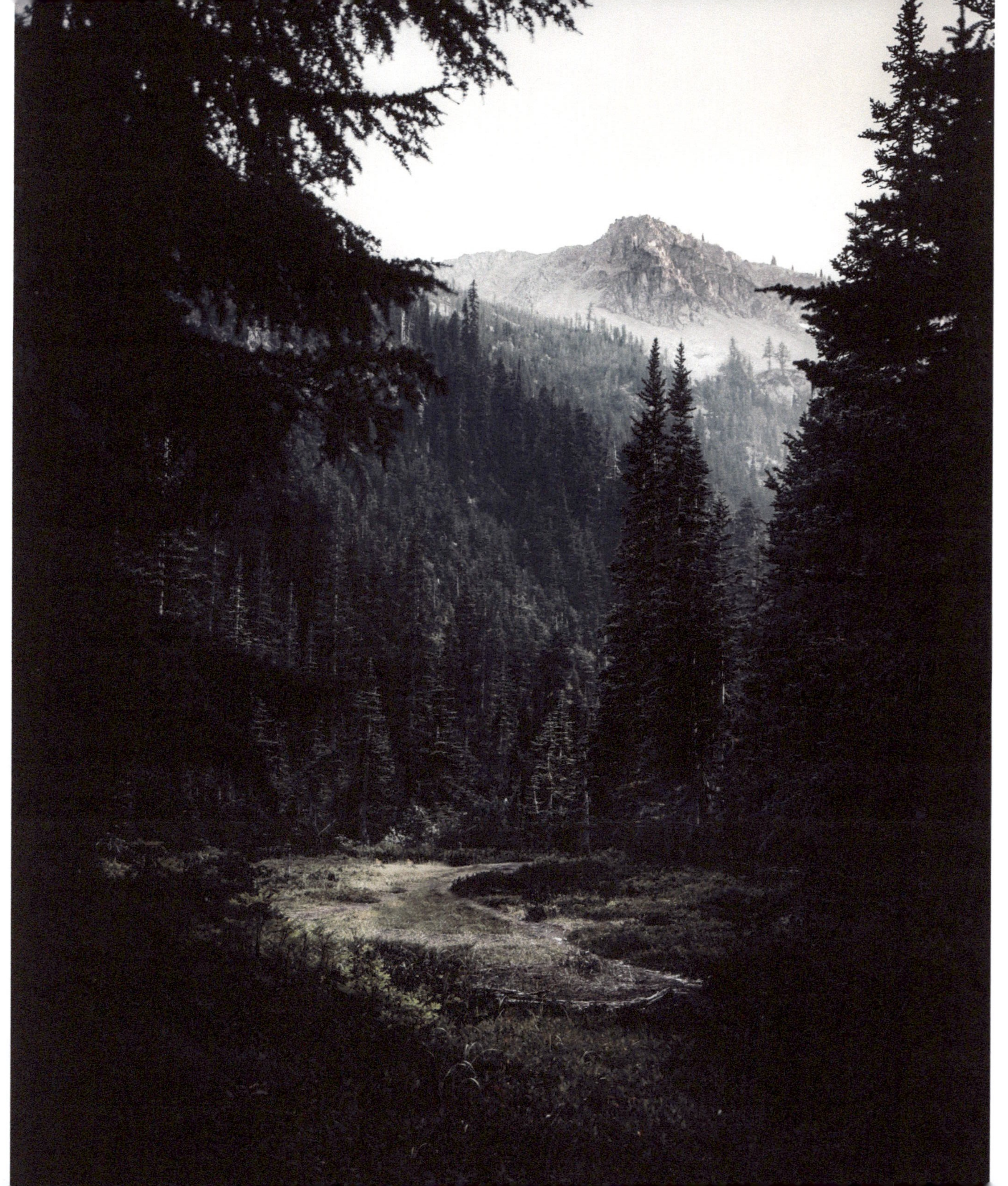

There's something wild about this place.
It feels mysterious and unpredictable.

It looks inviting yet foreboding.

The trees are speaking. They tower over me, scorning my presence.
They stand straight and tall with their silent message,
catching the wind in their short needles.

I can faintly smell the smell of Christmas trees and I instantly imagine
being gathered round a small fire with friends and family
on Christmas eve.

The sun has set now.
Darkness will be creeping into the valley soon.

The last person I saw on the trail was hours ago. My only companions
now are the menacing trees and the occasional bird or butterfly
inspecting nearby wildflowers.

I glance over my shoulder at the thought of a bear.

It's getting late now.
The trail is long, and the light is fading.
Yet, I can't bring myself to leave this place.
The aura it gives off is too compelling.
Just one last photo to capture the moment.

•

You will never know what you are capable of
doing and discovering if you never choose to push your limits.
God has called us higher and deeper, but we will never reach our full
potential if we never choose to take those
first steps of faith.

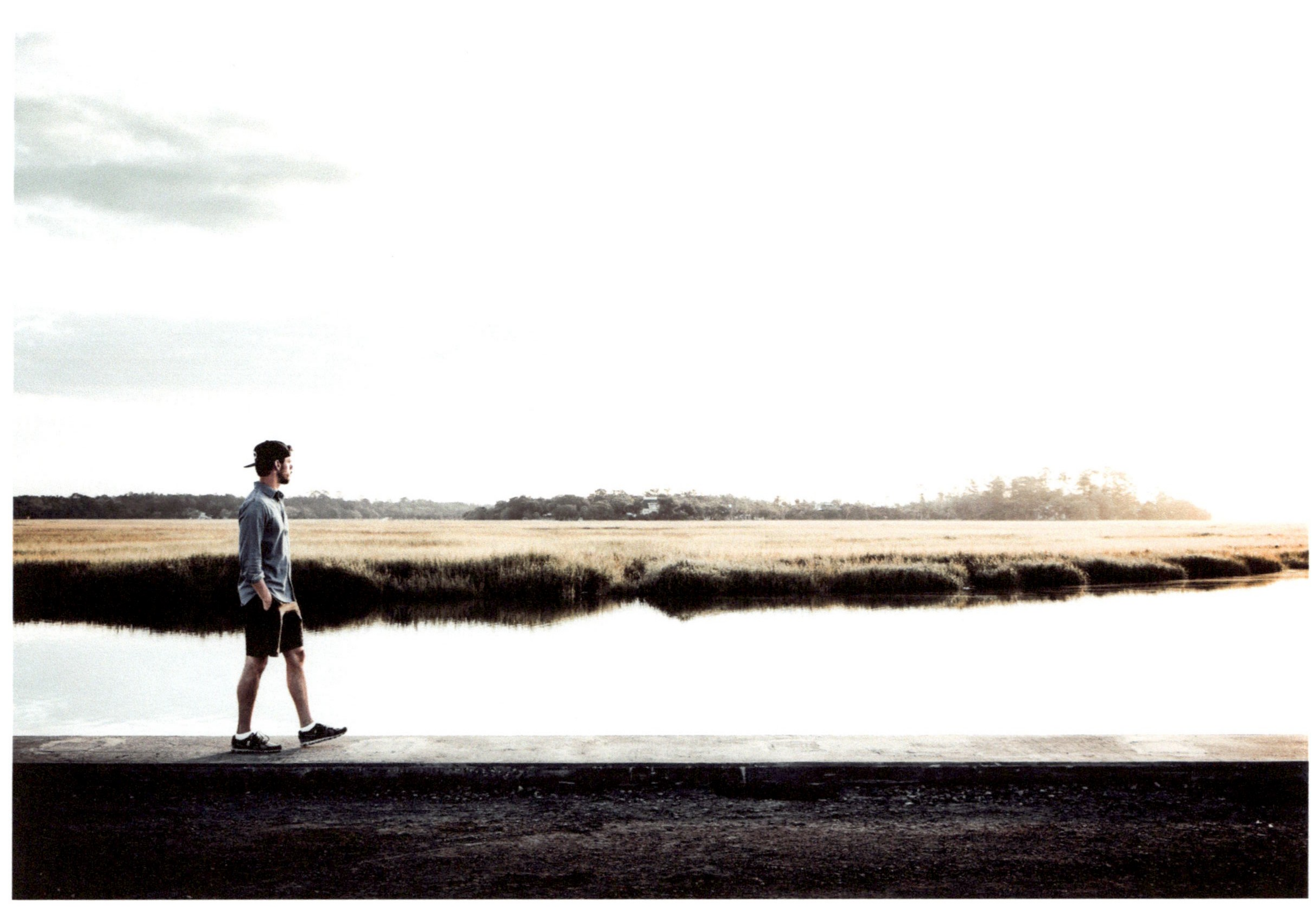

"The true test of a person's spiritual life and character is not what he does in the extraordinary moments of life, but what he does during the ordinary times when there is nothing tremendous or exciting happening. A person's worth is revealed in his attitude toward the ordinary things of life when he is not under the spotlight."
– Oswald Chambers

35°47'47"N   82°57'28"W

<u>Forgiveness</u>

"To forgive is to set a prisoner free and discover that the prisoner was you."
– Lewis B. Smedes

•
And sometimes, the hardest person to forgive is
the one standing in the mirror.

There are many times when I find myself trapped in a prison of my own making.
It may not be made of iron bars and concrete walls but rather unforgiveness, shame, and despair.
All too often, we choose to remain in unlocked cages simply because we cannot accept the fact that we are indeed
forgiven. We may know and believe in our hearts that Jesus offers forgiveness and even others may offer their own
forgiveness, but shame would hold us prisoner and keep us from reaching our full potential.

God has forgiven you. Can you forgive you?

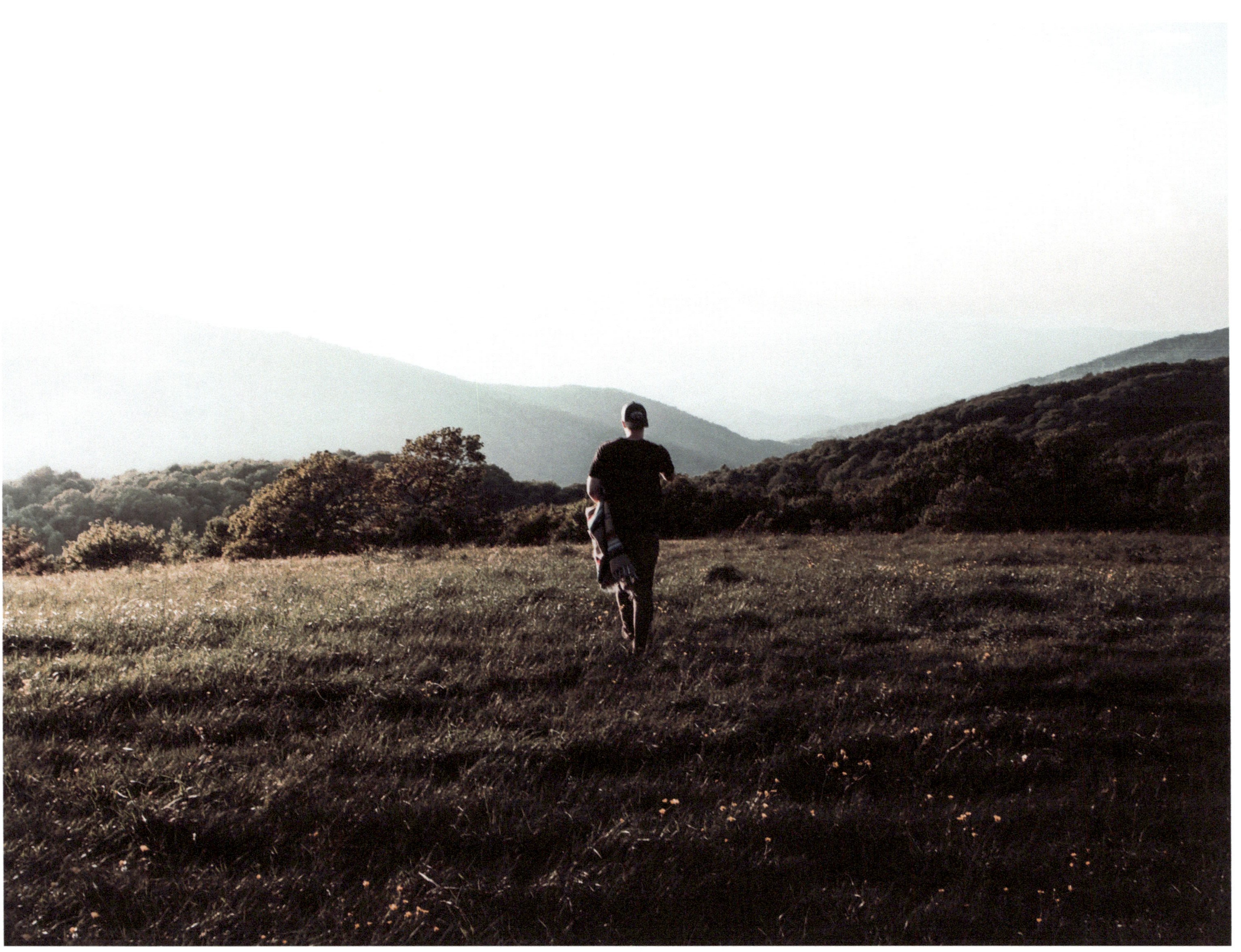

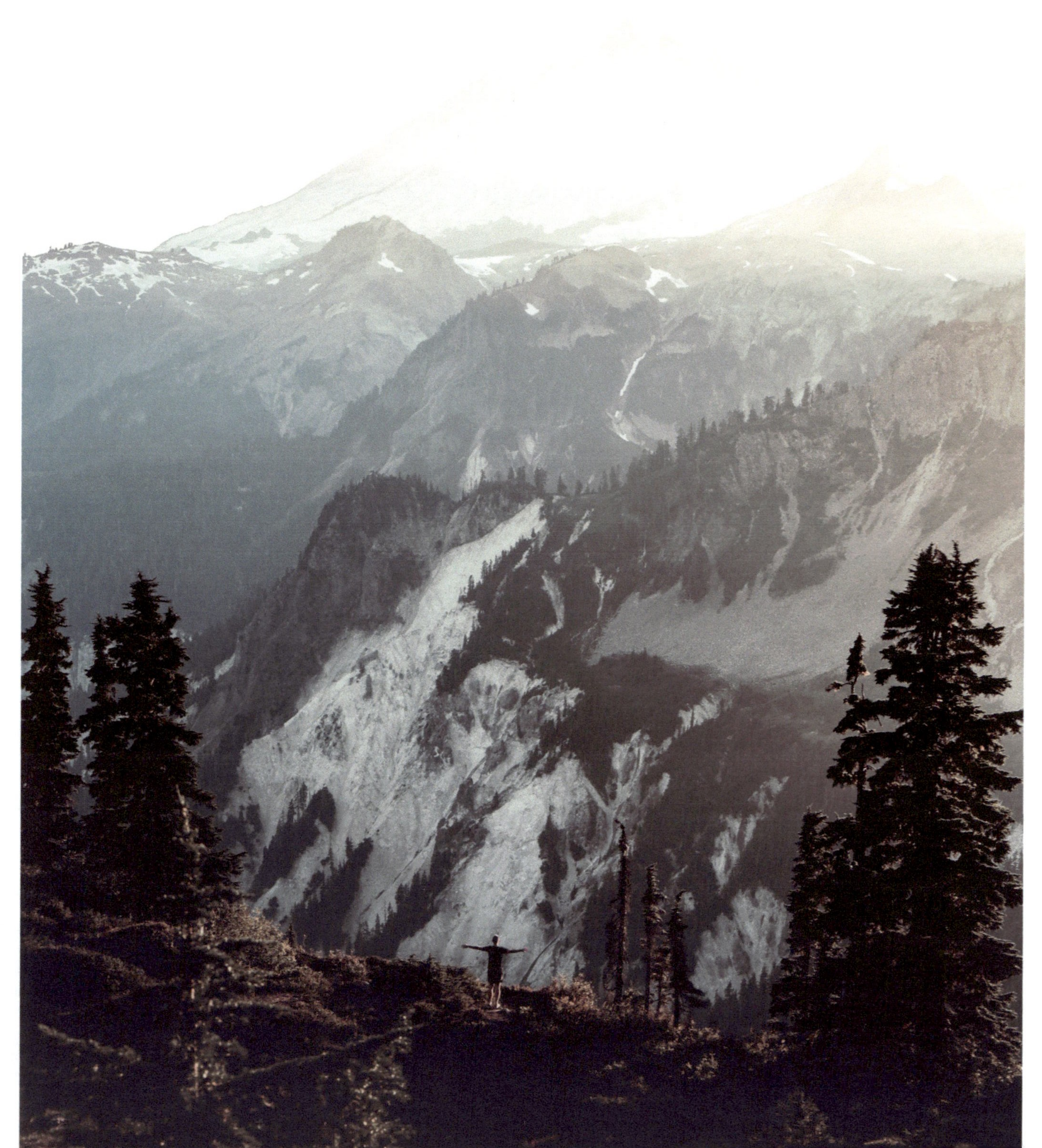

48°50'33"N 121°41'08"W

"Who is this that obscures my plans
with words without knowledge?
Brace yourself like a man;
I will question you, and you shall answer me.

Where were you when I laid the foundations of the earth?"

"Have you ever given orders to the morning,
or shown the dawn its place?"

"Does the hawk take flight by your wisdom
and spread its wings toward the south?
Does the eagle soar at your command
and build its nest on high?"

The Lord reigns, he is robed in majesty;
the Lord is robed in majesty and armed with strength.

"All these things my hand has made, and so all these things came to be,"
declares the Lord.
"But this is the one to whom I will look:
he who is humble and contrite in spirit and trembles at my word."

Job 38 | Job 39 | Psalm 93 | Isaiah 66

46°55'10"N   121°39'39"W

I have often found that my moments of greatest physical exertion are my
moments of greatest clarity

•

The precise moment in which you reach your limitations is the moment
in which you discover that you are indeed finite and in total dependence on the
One who sustains and orders all things.

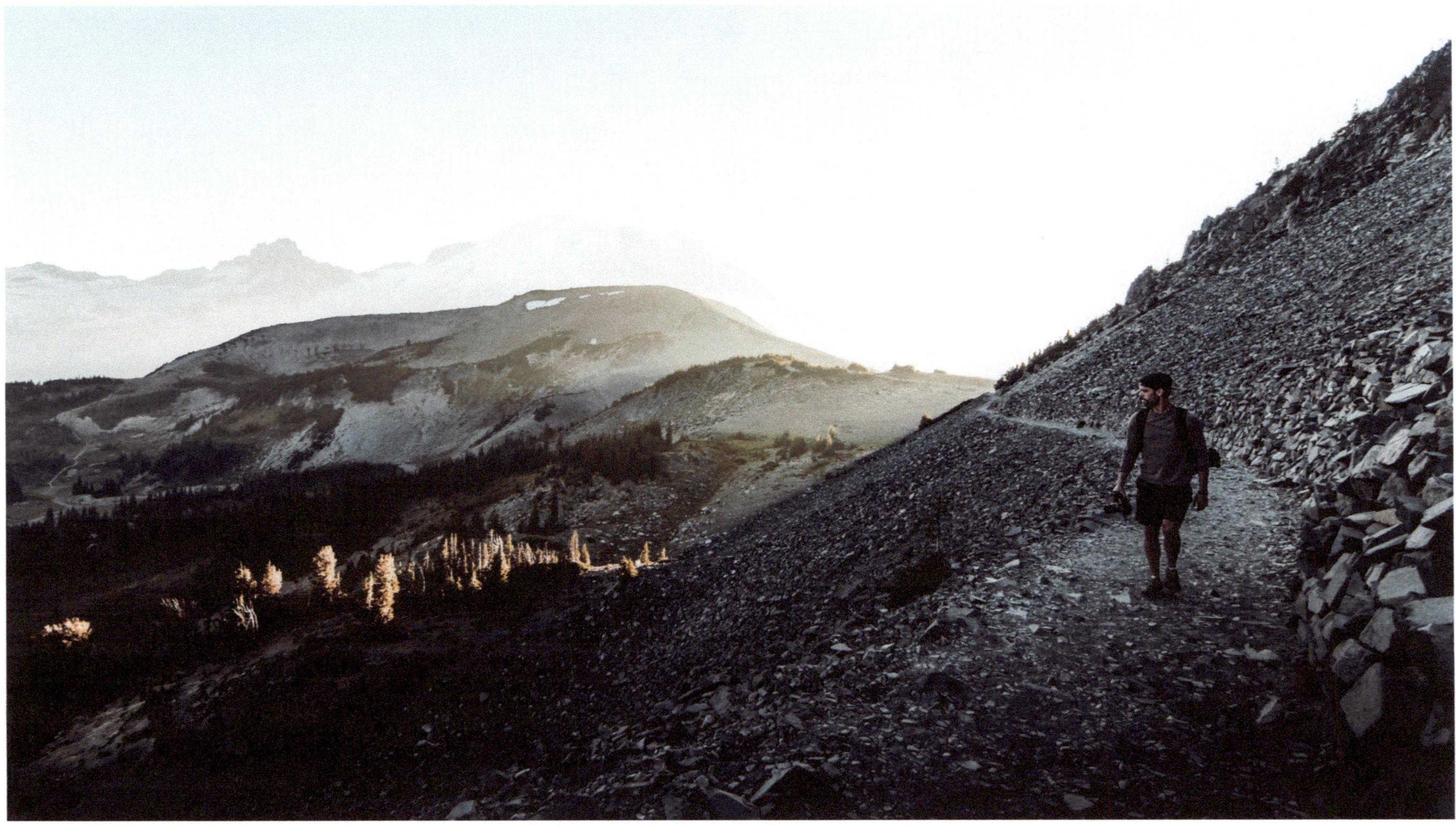

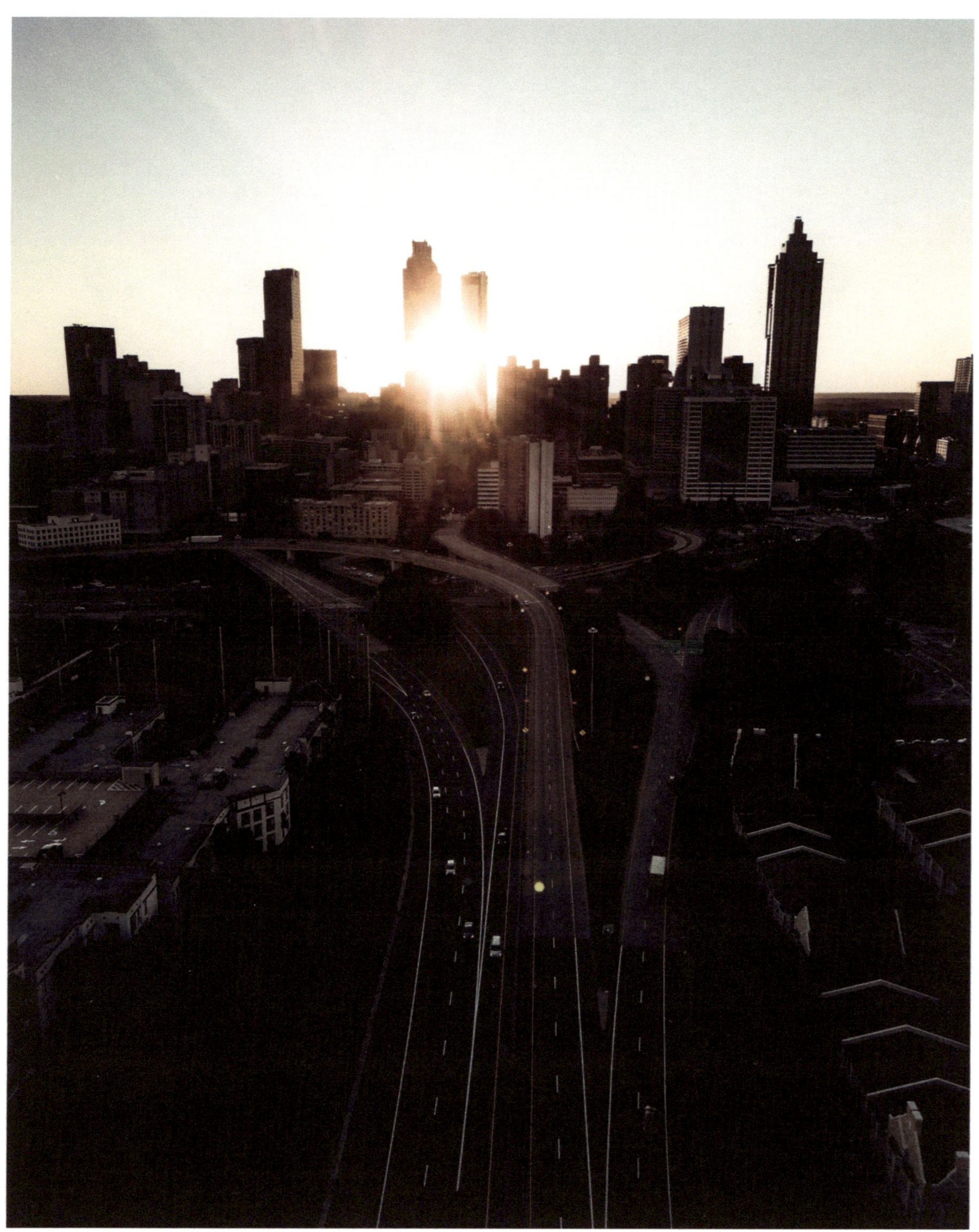

"All things are for your sakes, that grace, having SPREAD through the many, may cause thanksgiving to abound to the glory of God."
– II Corinthians 4:15

•

The phrase, "having spread through the many" catches my attention as I reflect on the idea that God often uses His people to extend and spread His grace to others causing thanksgiving and praise to abound. Very much in the same way a virus spreads from host to host causing sickness and death, God's grace also spreads from person to person causing thanksgiving and freedom. This then raises the question in my mind of

"What am I spreading?"

"What am I filling myself with?"

We speak of physical viruses that spread and the remedies to curb them. But why stop there? Fear is also a kind of virus. Bitterness? Envy? Strife?

These are viruses of the heart that we are all guilty of spreading at one point or another and the enemy would seek to fill our minds with cares of this world to hinder, distract, and dampen the impact of God's grace in us and through us. The enemy would have us crippled by sickness. The good news is that while viruses destroy, God's grace heals.

Yet, many times, the choice of what we allow our minds to dwell on and be filled with is up to us. The assurance is that His grace always abounds and is always ready to displace the sickness. One moves out as the other moves in, and you can be sure that whatever you carry, you will spread.

46°55'30"N   121°40'29"W

"God's training is for now, not later. His purpose is for this very minute, not for
sometime in the future. We have nothing to do with what will follow our obedience,
and we are wrong to concern ourselves with it. What people call preparation,
God sees as the goal itself."
– Oswald Chambers

•

We must learn to be more present in the here and now,
and remember that the process is not a thing to blindly get through as fast as possible
and forget, but rather something to embrace and take moment by moment in total
dependence on the one who leads.

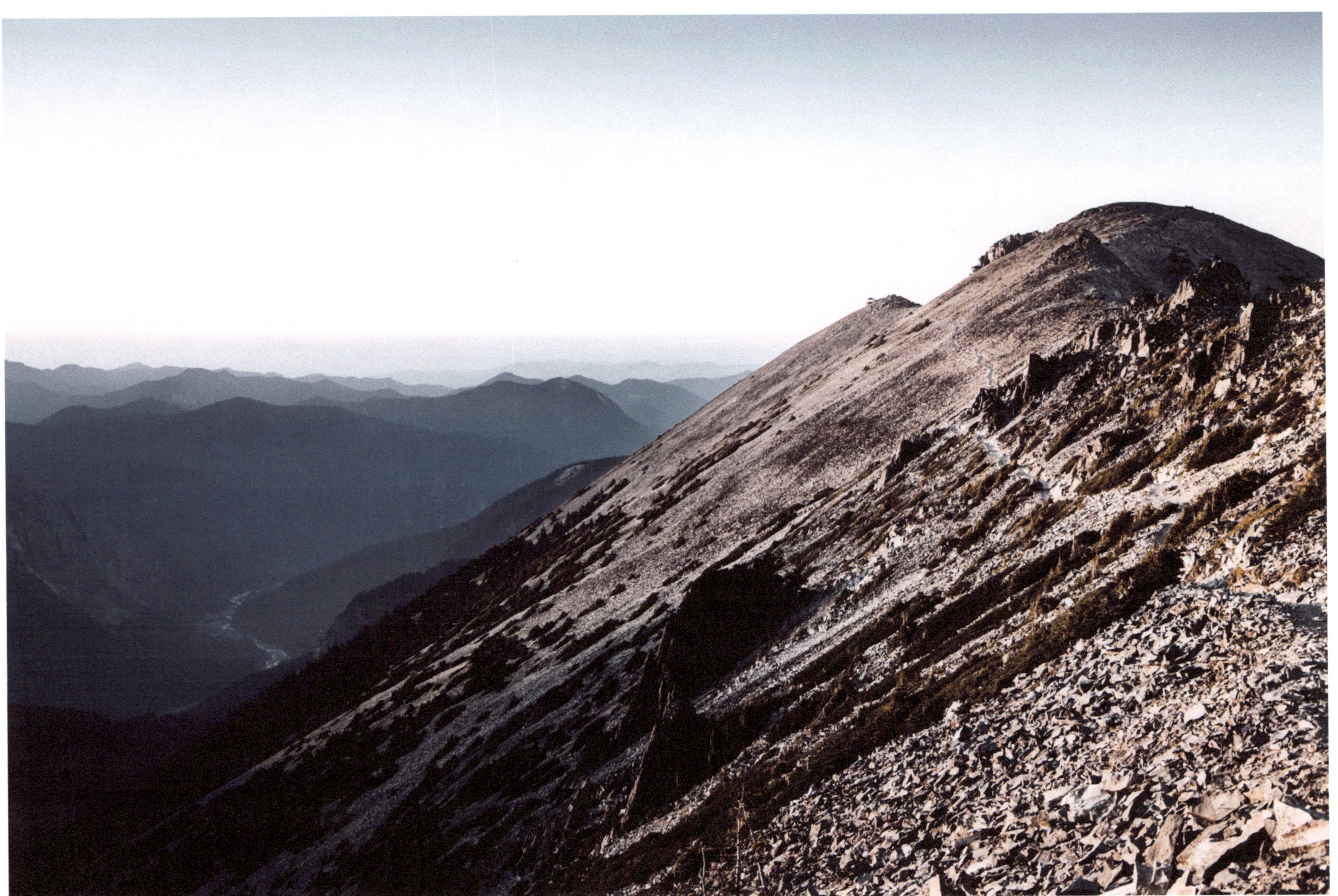

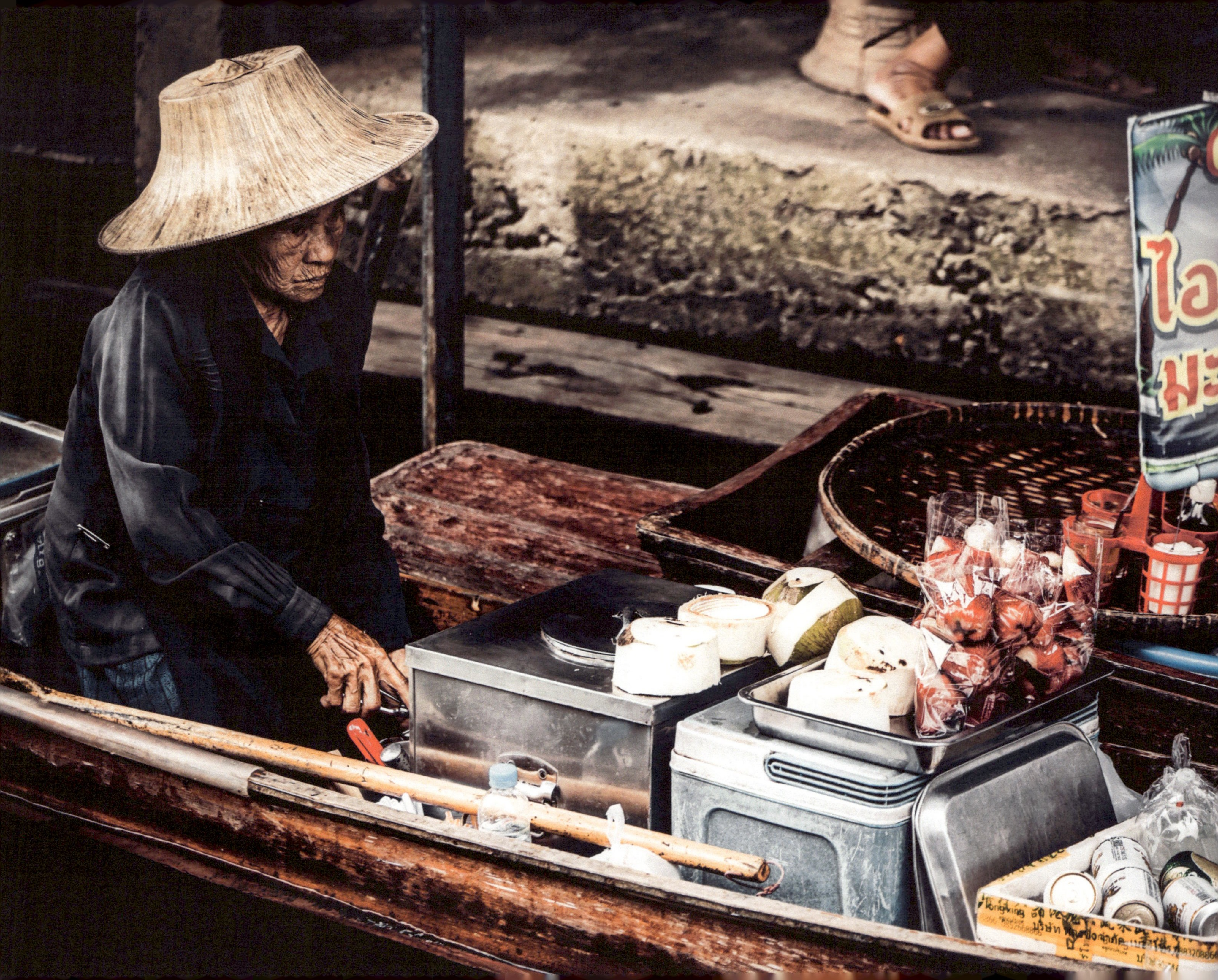
ไอ
มะ

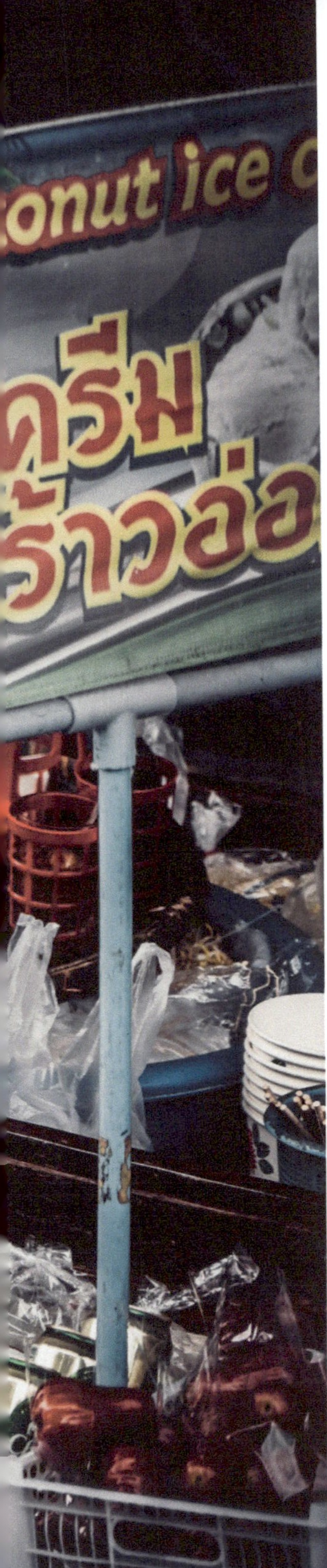

13°31'16"N 99°57'31"E

The heart of man is searching. The heart of God stands ready
with arms stretched out.

Sometimes, mountains come in the form of
a man's heart.

48°57'23"N 121°38'35"W

<u>Behold</u>

"See, I am doing a new thing!
Now it springs up; do you not perceive it? I am making a way in the wilderness
and streams in the wasteland."
– Isaiah 43:19

"...forgetting what is behind and straining toward what is ahead,"
– Philippians 3:13

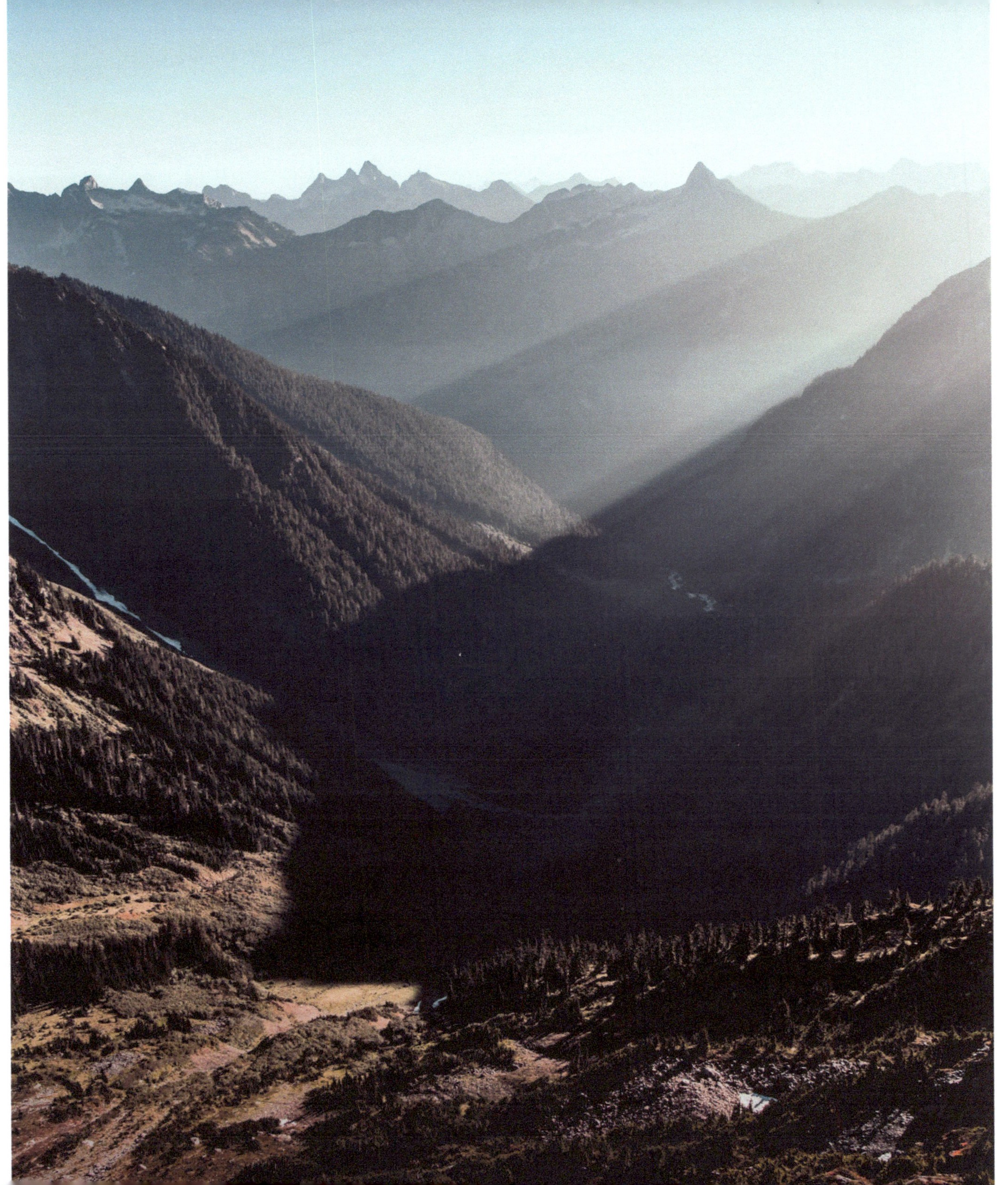

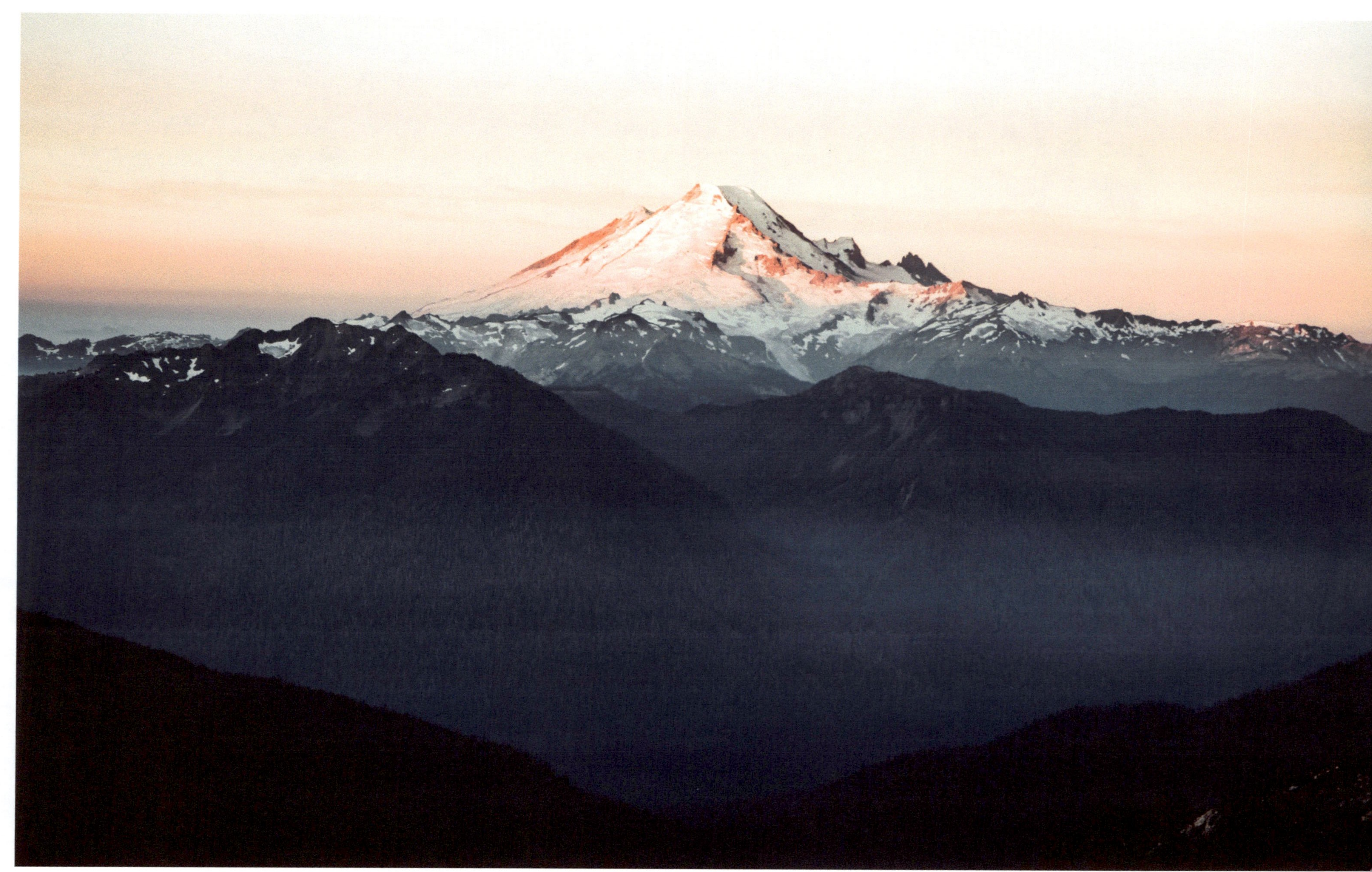

48°50'32"N 121°41'11"W

On the mountain of the LORD, it will be provided.
— Genesis 22:14

"If I find in myself a desire which no other experience in this world can satisfy, the most probable explanation is that I was made for another world."
— C. S. Lewis, Mere Christianity

•

Buried deep within the heart of man is a longing to explore and discover new horizons.
To never venture beyond the borders of our own restrictive comfort zones would be a tragedy indeed.
However, the greater tragedy would be to explore in search of fulfillment, but never discover the
One who called us in the beginning and birthed within us the desire and longing for more
which only He can satisfy.

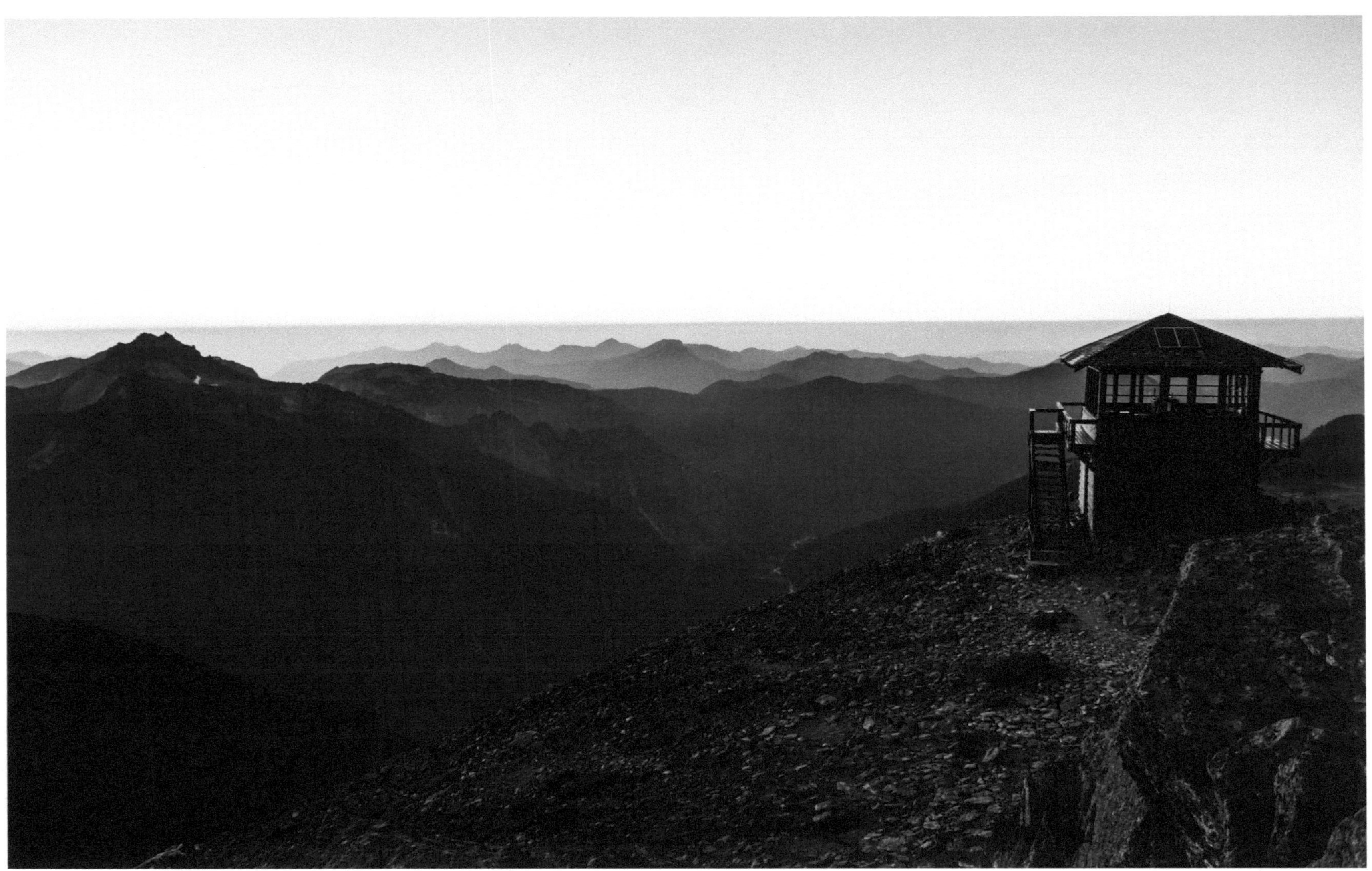

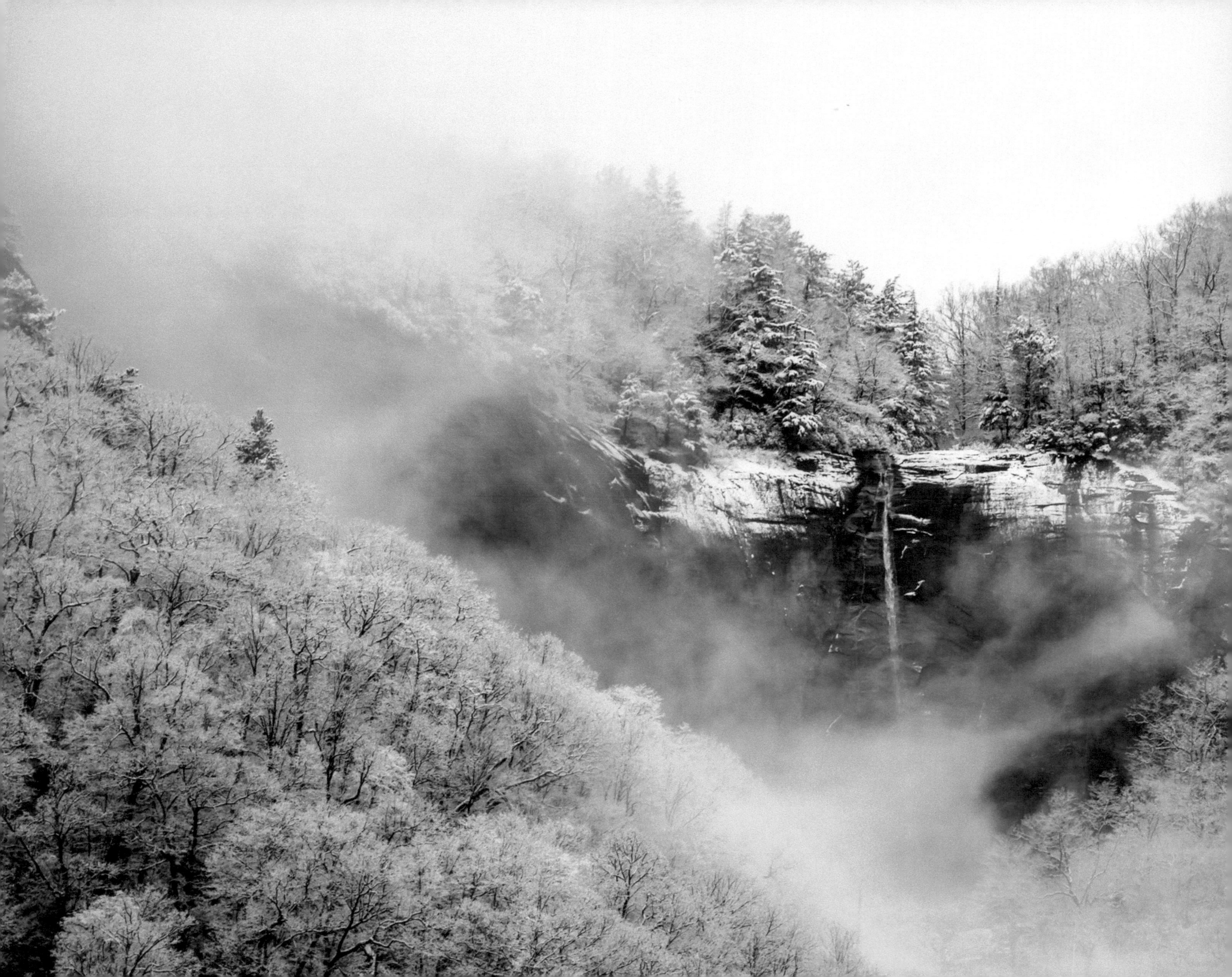

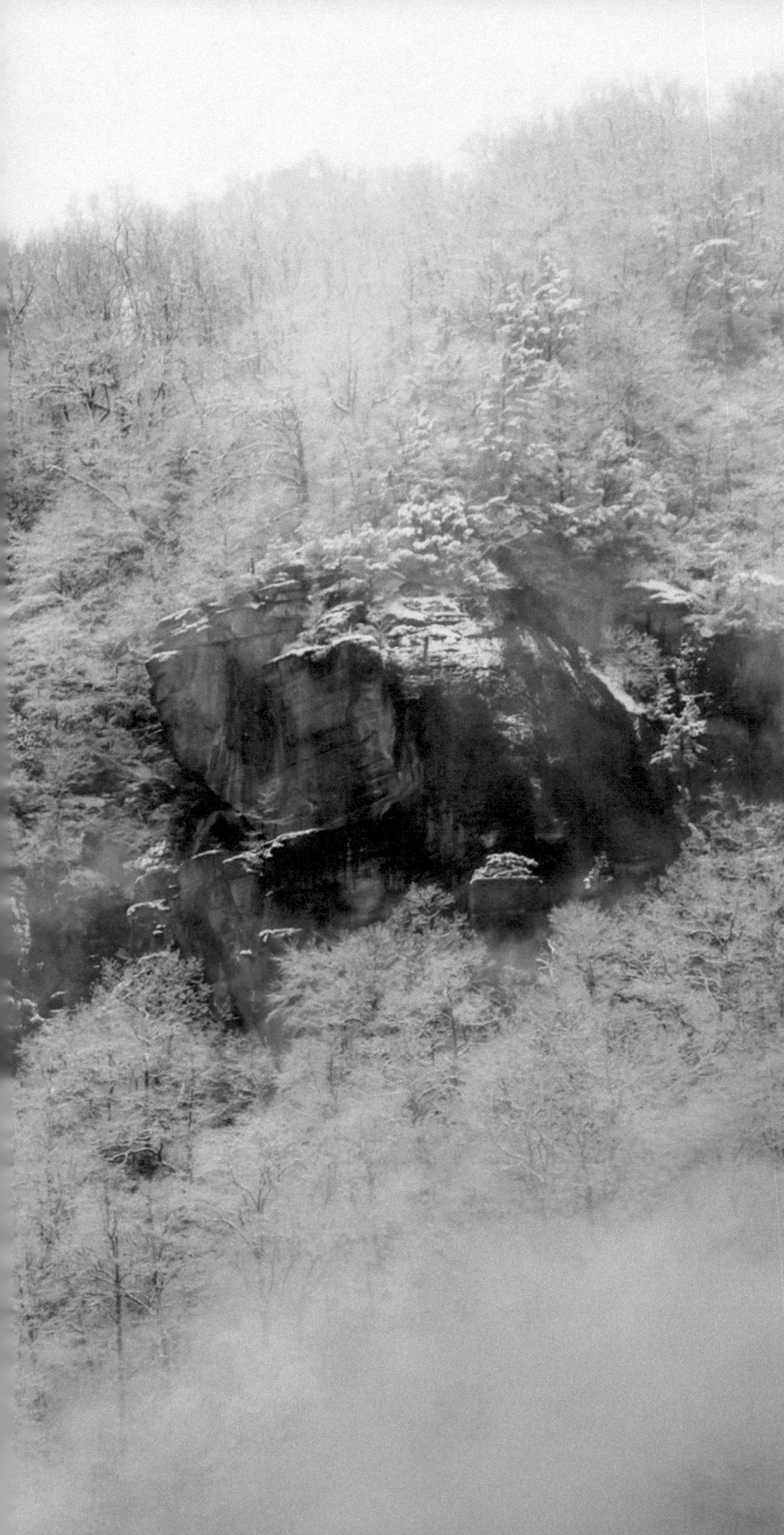

God's timing is often not our own and, many times,
He chooses not to give us what we first want when we want it.

Sometimes, He withholds simply because He knows that what we want will not be
good for us, and just as a father knows what is best for his children so the LORD knows
what is best for those who fear Him. Other times, He withholds because if we will only
wait for just a little while He will give us something far greater
than we could have thought or imagined.

This wintry photo is a standing testament to that truth.
Had I captured the photo that I thought I wanted upon my first visit, I would have
never returned to this place to witness this moment of a snow-covered landscape
draped in drifting fog.

Upon my first attempt to capture the falls, the adverse weather conditions made it
impossible for me to catch even a short glimpse of the landscape. I came away that
day feeling beaten and discouraged without a single image of the falls on my camera.

But the story didn't end there.

Due to my lack of success on my previous visit, I decided to give it another try.
Little did I know what God had prepared for me. I knew there was a chance of flurries
and possibly light snow during the night but when I awoke that morning and stepped
outside, heaps of freshly fallen snow had covered everything around me.

I was ecstatic.

I had hoped for a view of the falls under a moody sky but I never imagined capturing
these conditions, especially at this location. I went a short distance to my planned
vantage point and there lay the falls, nestled away in the corner of the forest atop the
snow-covered cliffs. The fog ever so elegantly framed and reframed the scene as the
falls drifted in and out of view.

Had I been allowed to capture the photo I thought I wanted on my first
attempt, I would have never returned to witness this rare
moment for this location.

Wait on the LORD. Trust Him.
He knows best and His timing is perfect.

EXPLORE | DISCOVER | CREATE | INSPIRE

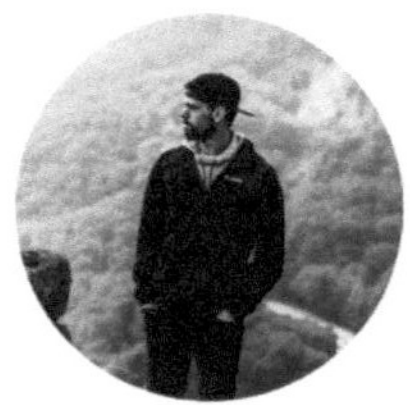

All photographs are available for purchase at
www.studio124.tv
or upon specific request at
scook@studio124.tv